MIGUEL NUNEZ
2 PETER & JUDE
FOR YOU

CONTENTS

SERIES PREFACE

Each volume of the *God's Word For You* series takes you to the heart of a book of the Bible, and applies its truths to your heart.

The central aim of each title is to be:

- Bible centered
- Christ glorifying
- Relevantly applied
- Easily readable

You can use *2 Peter and Jude For You:*

To read. You can simply read from cover to cover, as a book that explains and explores the themes, encouragements and challenges of this part of Scripture.

To feed. You can work through this book as part of your own personal regular devotions, or use it alongside a sermon or Bible-study series at your church. Each chapter is divided into two (or occasionally three) shorter sections, with questions for reflection at the end of each.

To lead. You can use this as a resource to help you teach God's word to others, both in small-group and whole-church settings. You'll find tricky verses or concepts explained using ordinary language, and helpful themes and illustrations along with suggested applications.

These books are not commentaries. They assume no understanding of the original Bible languages, nor a high level of biblical knowledge. Verse references are marked in **bold** so that you can refer to them easily. Any words that are used rarely or differently in everyday language outside the church are marked in gray when they first appear, and are explained in a glossary toward the back. There, you'll also find details of resources you can use alongside this one, in both personal and church life.

Our prayer is that as you read, you'll be struck not by the contents of this book, but by the book it's helping you open up; and that you'll praise not the author of this book, but the One he is pointing you to.

Carl Laferton, Series Editor

Bible translations used:

NIV: New International Version (this is the version being quoted unless otherwise stated)

NLT: New Living Translation

ESV: English Standard Version

INTRODUCTION TO 2 PETER & JUDE

Over recent years we have witnessed the fall of a significant number of church leaders from many different backgrounds. The reasons have varied from one case to another, but often there have been issues of illicit sexuality, mishandling of finances, abuse of power and authority, and substance abuse, among a few others.

Every single case has been sad and painful. Yes, painful is the right word. These leaders have been looked up to by many as examples of godliness and gifting. When they fall away so catastrophically, we wonder what is going on. What happened to them? How did they start drifting? Didn't God warn them ahead of time? Of course, God did! I am sure he did—more than once and in more than one way. They just refused to pay attention to the warning signs. They refused to heed the apostle Paul's advice: "So, if you think you are standing firm, be careful that you don't fall!" (1 Corinthians 10:12).

Many of these leaders were running the Christian race well at some point in their lives; but then they stumbled and fell. And this is something that could happen to any one of us—church leaders and church members alike—however well we are running today.

The reality is that these failures of faith and morality have been happening since the birth of the church and even before. Peter and Jude knew that first-hand. The brothers and sisters they were writing to were new believers, and they were experiencing persecution; in those circumstances, they had fallen under the influence of false teachers, who were sexually immoral, financially greedy and power-hungry. A terrible combination for a newborn church! The two letters that this book explores, 2 Peter and Jude, show a deep concern for the future of the faith of the believing communities they are addressing. Peter and Jude write with an intense sense of urgency about the danger of apostasy* under the pressure of wrong teaching and immoral leaders. They write to help their readers to stand firm.

---

* Words in gray are defined in the Glossary (page 147).

The danger of stumbling is as real today as it has been throughout the course of human history. Our generation is especially vulnerable to moral temptations which come to us via television and social media—temptations which are accessible, anonymous and affordable. We are also constantly bombarded with ideas totally contrary to the word of God from every part of our culture. The internet offers all kinds of teachings, bad as well as good, 24 hours a day.

Lies even come from within the church itself. In the last two or three decades we have seen the spread around the globe of the prosperity gospel—whose preachers promise material blessing from God. We have seen the adoption of pragmatism into the heart of churches, tempting us to think that what makes an activity worthwhile or not is the impact it has rather than what Scripture says about it. We have seen the "name it and claim it" movement, in which people are taught that there is power in our words to convert our desires into reality. We have heard teachers of the word undermining the value of God's law in favor of a super-grace that sounds more like license to sin. There are also issues surrounding social justice—an important topic, yet one which, if approached from the wrong angle, may threaten the centrality of the gospel.

As you can see, Satan never ceases to find a way to attack the church of Jesus Christ. He is doing what he has done since the very beginning—trying to divert our attention from the truth and lure us away from our God. When someone falls away—whether that shows itself in their false teachings or in their moral failings—they have believed Satan's lies.

Truth and the Church

Pastor and theologian John Stott once wrote, "The church's greatest troublemakers (now as then) are not those outside who oppose, ridicule and persecute it, but those inside who try to change the gospel" (*The Message of Galatians*, p 23). If we lose the gospel, we lose the church, because the former leads to the latter. Truth is what anchors the church. This is why the apostle Paul fought so hard to maintain the purity of the gospel message:

"I am astonished that you are so quickly deserting the one who called you to live in the grace of Christ and are turning to a different gospel—which is really no gospel at all. Evidently some people are throwing you into confusion and are trying to pervert the gospel of Christ. But even if we or an angel from heaven should preach a gospel other than the one we preached to you, let them be under God's curse! As we have already said, so now I say again: If anybody is preaching to you a gospel other than what you accepted, let them be under God's curse!" (Galatians 1:6-9)

Once truth has become negotiable, we can easily predict the consequences: division (which happened in the early church at Corinth); loss of the gospel (at Galatia); philosophical ideas becoming attractive (at Colossae); weakening of the first love (at Ephesus); a personal relationship with Christ becoming mere religiosity (at Sardis); the faith becoming lukewarm (at Laodicea); and in time, believers falling away altogether. What begins as a distortion of doctrine changes our thinking; and sooner or later, a changed mind gives birth to a sinful or an immoral lifestyle.

Both Peter and Jude know the weight of the issue: the gospel is at stake, and so the salvation of men and women is also at stake. As we study these two letters, we will see that they are about the preservation of the truth and, therefore,

> These letters are about the preservation of the truth – and the preservation of the church.

the preservation of the church. In our day as in theirs, we need both men and women who are willing "to contend for the faith that was once for all entrusted to God's holy people" (Jude v 3).

Outlines and Authorship

Before we study these letters, there are a few important facts to note. Apparently, Origen (AD 184 – 253) was the first **Church Father** to endorse 2 Peter as a canonical letter—part of **inspired** Scripture. This late acceptance may seem like a bad sign; but, in reality, it is good to know that the early church was careful and took its time in deciding the canonicity of each book of the Bible. It's clear that Peter is the author—he says so (1:1), and he also alludes to experiences we know Peter had (1:16-18). According to tradition, Peter was crucified upside down by the Emperor Nero, who died in AD 68. Therefore, this letter must have been written before that time. Most believe that it was probably written around AD 67.

Here is a brief outline of 2 Peter:

1. Salutation (1:1-2)

2. Standing firm in what you know (1:3-21)

3. Standing firm against false teachers (2:1-22)

4. Standing firm until the Lord returns (3:1-18)

Regarding the **epistle** of Jude, we have some early evidence to believe that the author, who identifies himself as "Jude, a servant of Jesus Christ and a brother of James" (1:1), was the half-brother of Jesus. Some discussions have occurred since the early-church era regarding the letter's canonicity, especially since Jude quotes some nonbiblical sources (Jude v 9, 14-15). However, it was accepted as canonical and ascribed to Jude as early as the 2nd century (see Elmer L. Towns and Ben Gutierrez, *The Essence of the New Testament*, p 319). It is judged to have been written between AD 60 and 70, on the basis that "scoffers are referred to as future in 2 Peter 3:3 and they are present in Jude 18" (Norman L. Geisler, *A Popular Survey of the New Testament*, p 305).

Here is a brief outline of Jude:

1. Contending for the faith (v 1-7)

2. Condemnation for the false teachers (v 8-16)

3. Certainty of salvation until the end (v 17-25)

When it comes to our Christian walk, remaining on track is, on one level, the responsibility of each one of us. Peter says, "Make every effort to confirm your calling and election. For if you do [the things he has just listed], you will never stumble" (2 Peter 1:10). But at another level, finishing well is the work of God in us. Jude acknowledges that "kept for Jesus Christ" (Jude v 1): God is the one, in the end, who can keep us from stumbling (v 24). It is through pursuing him, and throwing ourselves on his mercy, that we will make it to the end of the race—to be presented before his glorious throne "without fault and with great joy" (v 24).

It is important, as you begin, to approach these letters as being fully inspired by God, which makes them inerrant and infallible; to pray for illumination of your understanding by the Spirit; to adopt a humble and teachable attitude; and to decide to obey their content. God will then bless the studying of his word.

1. HOW TO KEEP FROM STUMBLING

In the first chapter of his letter, Peter begins by helping us see how to run the race of the Christian life well. The final words of this first section read, "If you do these things, you will never stumble, and you will receive a rich welcome into the eternal kingdom of our Lord and Savior Jesus Christ" (2 Peter **1:10-11***). This is what Peter is leading up to throughout **1:1-11**.

Peter writes with a sense of urgency and intensity. It's important to know why. What was happening was that false teachers were seeking to entice true disciples away from their Savior. Peter is desperate to ensure that the believers will not follow this dangerous path. He wants them to make it to the "rich welcome" that is waiting for them if they remain faithful to their Lord.

In 2:20-22, Peter will speak about how these false teachers had denied the holy commandment. Apparently, from what could be seen on the surface, these **apostates** had experienced salvation—or, at least, had been involved in some sort of encounter that led them to believe that they were in a state of salvation. In other words, they had seemed on the surface to accept Jesus as Lord. However, even after enjoying the Lord's blessings, they had gone back to involving themselves in the corruption and pleasures of this world. Peter refers to these people as being blind: they had forgotten about the purification of their sins, which they had experienced the moment they believed (**1:9**).

---

* All 2 Peter and Jude verse references being looked at in each chapter part are in **bold**.

As we read further along in 2 Peter, we begin to realize that the group being discussed here had abandoned Christian morality. They had embraced sexual immorality, drunkenness, and gluttony (2:13). These men lived without law. They were rebelling against the Lord's commandments. In 2:19, Peter says they are nothing more than slaves of corruption—yet at the same time they are promising freedom to those who follow their teaching.

These pretenders inside the church did not take a passive stand; they actively tried to win over the disciples to their way of thinking and behaving. Their sinful practices were founded on untrue teachings about God, and they sought to persuade others to believe those teachings. They argued that the future judgment would never take place, and as a result they denied that the Lord would come in judgment (3:3-4). You can see why that would lead them to embrace immoral behavior; if there was to be no justice in the end, there was no obligation to act justly now.

This combination of heretical doctrine and sinful behavior was proving seductive, especially to those who were "unstable"—perhaps new believers or those who were especially tempted by particular sins such as sexual immorality. Peter was deeply concerned that those who were weak in the faith might be dragged away to follow the false teachers' lies. He knew that if these practices were allowed—and this is true of any church at any time—the end result would not only be the introduction of heresy but also the destruction of the overall stability of the congregation. This is why Peter is writing his letter.

Making Introductions

As soon as we begin to read, we notice that the author identifies himself by his first name, which was typical of 1st-century letters: "Simon Peter, a servant and apostle of Jesus Christ" (**1:1**). Simon, which was his original name, comes from the Hebrew language; it was a very familiar and common name in 1st-century Israel. But

Christ himself renamed Simon with the Greek name Peter, which means "rock" (he is also called "Cephas," which is the Aramaic word for the same thing). Here, both names are being used—"Simon Peter"—which was not unusual at that time.

Peter calls himself "a servant and apostle of Jesus Christ." "Servant" is the translation of the Greek word *doulos*, which literally means "slave." Peter is referring to himself as a slave of Jesus Christ. But he is not trying to show humility, necessarily. Rather, the word "slave" conveys the idea of belonging to someone else—and in this case to our Lord Jesus Christ. In ancient Israel, the word was sometimes used of slaves who could have gone free during the Year of Jubilee (see Leviticus 25) but decided to stay with their owner out of love (Exodus 21:5-6). Perhaps this is the type of slavery Peter has in mind.

The word "apostle" denotes those chosen by Christ and charged with the responsibility of leading the early church. Peter is not trying to demonstrate superiority over anyone by using this word. Rather, he is emphasizing that he has the authority to write this letter.

Next, Peter identifies his audience: "Those who through the righteousness of our God and Savior Jesus Christ have received a faith as precious as ours" (2 Peter **1:1**). Peter is aware that even though he is an apostle, the quality and caliber of his faith is no different from that of the rest of us—who have also believed as he did. Our faith is "as precious as" that of the apostles.

In passing, Peter explains how we received our faith: "by the righteousness of our God and Savior Jesus Christ." In other words, we have not received faith through our works or our own merits. Rather, we have received this faith as a gift of grace from Jesus Christ himself, who went to the cross and shed blood on our behalf. This sets us apart from any false teachers who say that salvation is obtained by some special knowledge that others do not have (as Gnostics believed in the 1st century) or through works of merit. As true disciples of Jesus Christ, we do work to be righteous; but we do it after being empowered by grace. It is through Jesus that we receive righteousness.

In **verse 2**, Peter greets the recipients of the letter by using the expression "grace and peace." Peter helps us to see that grace and peace are received as the result of the redeeming work of Christ: "in the knowledge of God and of Jesus our Lord." Without this knowledge, there is no possible way to enjoy these blessings to which Peter is referring. With it, they are ours "in abundance."

God's Promises for Our Walk

What follows is an extraordinary revelation from the writing of the apostle Peter. "His divine power has given us everything we need for a godly life through our knowledge of him who called us by his own glory and goodness" (**v 3**). The day we are born again, we are blessed beyond measure in two different ways. We are not only saved from the wrath of God; we are also equipped by God to live the life we have just received. Since we do not possess in ourselves the power to grow in holiness, God sends his Spirit—the Spirit of Christ (Romans 8:9)—to dwell within us. We no longer simply have "God with us," but, even better, God *within* us. This is the Spirit who empowers all of us as believers to live a life worthy of our calling—a life in which we turn away from sin and draw nearer to God. We were called from worldliness to godliness—that is, to a moral life that honors God.

The power to live in such a distinctive manner has been received "through our knowledge of him who called us by his own glory and goodness" (2 Peter **1:3**). The more we know God in Christ, the more we become like him. God has provided *everything* we need to live a victorious life to the very end as we follow the Spirit's leading.

But if our growth in the knowledge of God stagnates, we return to the practices we had before we were redeemed. The Christian who does not live a life of moral excellence is resisting the power of the Spirit dwelling within them. This is the main cause of our failures.

God has given promises to those who believe in him, and these promises have the power to aid us in our walk with him. This truth appears in the very next verse. Our God "has given us his very great and precious promises, so that through them you may participate in the divine nature, having escaped the corruption in the world caused by evil desires" (**v 4**). The New Living Translation (NLT) expresses it this way: "These are the promises that enable you to share his divine nature and escape the world's corruption caused by human desires." In other words, if we as Christians truly come to trust in the promises the Lord has given us, we will see that they are an enormous help as we face the difficulties and temptations of this world.

Hebrews 11 gives many examples of this. It refers to the joyful end of the Old Testament heroes, who trusted in the promises of God and as a result did not waver in their faith. They saw the things God had promised from afar and "welcomed them from a distance, admitting that they were foreigners and strangers on earth" (Hebrews 11:13). When we trust God with all our heart and mind, his promises are an encouragement to us—serving, as it were, as a faith fertilizer or an empowering tool so that we may endure suffering as we carry out God's purposes. **Abraham** is a particularly good example: "By faith Abraham, when God tested him, offered **Isaac** as a sacrifice. He who had *embraced the promises* was about to sacrifice his one and only son" (Hebrews 11:17, emphasis added). If Abraham was capable of being such a great witness while living under the **old covenant**, just by believing in God's promises, how much more should we be able to live a life of faith now that we have

> God's promises are a faith fertilizer, an empowering tool.

received a wider revelation and "better promises" (Hebrews 8:6)? To put it bluntly, by comparison with **Job, Moses, Jeremiah,** and **Daniel**—just to mention a few—we are wimps.

Given what we have learned in the initial four verses of this letter, we can see two reasons why believers compromise their Christian walk:

- They stop growing in the knowledge of God (2 Peter **1:3**).

- They forget the powerful promises Peter alludes to (**v 4**).

God knows very well the effect on us of the knowledge of himself and the understanding of his ways. To know God better is to grow in Christ-likeness.

So we must each ask ourselves: Am I growing? Or am I stagnating? How real are the promises of God to me?

Remember, through the power and the promises of God we have become partakers of God's divine nature and can escape "the corruption in the world caused by evil desires" (**v 4**). That reality makes the entire difference.

Questions for reflection

1. God has given us everything we need for a godly life. So why do you think believers can have such a difficult time living a life of obedience?

2. According to what we studied at the beginning of this chapter, what is the difference between the teachers of the true gospel and the teachers of the false gospel?

3. Which promises of God do you find yourself doubting? Why? How could you take hold of those promises today?

PART TWO

If there was ever someone who was capable of warning Christians about how to avoid stumbling, it was the apostle Peter. As Bible commentator Warren Wiersbe writes, Peter "had a tendency, in his early years, to feel overconfident when danger was near and to ignore the Master's warnings. He rushed ahead when he should have waited; he slept when he should have prayed; he talked when he should have listened. He was a courageous, but careless, Christian" (*The Exposition Bible Commentary*, p 436). This was the apostle who denied his Lord three times, disowning his best friend. No one is better equipped to warn others against the danger of stumbling or falling than one who has been through the experience. Himself a veteran of human failure, Peter wants to prevent these experiences from happening to his brothers and sisters in the faith. He is concerned about the possibility that false teachers might divert true believers off the path—so in **1:5-11**, he gives his readers the key to finishing their race well.

Peter begins by calling attention to the responsibility we have in our growing process: we are to "make every effort" (**v 5**). Many Christians believe that God will do everything for you once you are his child. But that is not the case. The degree to which God is close to the believer—and by "close" I do not mean how near he is geographically, but how much he manifests himself in your life—depends upon your degree of obedience to his will. This is why James tells us, "Come near to God and he will come near to you" (James 4:8).

The Ladder of Growth

Through the Spirit, God has provided us with everything we need to live virtuously. It is now up to us to develop and use what he has provided. This is why Peter speaks of adding "goodness" to our faith (2 Peter **1:5**): that is, moral excellence. We have been endowed with God's power, God's word, and God's Spirit to grow in our sanctification. Of course, we will never reach moral perfection this side of glory. But it is possible to live a life not characterized by sin but by righteousness (1 Peter 2:24). Moral excellence means walking in integrity of heart; when we sin (not if), we deal with our sin in humility and repentance, trusting in the grace of God, who brought not only the **conviction** of sin upon us but also the desire to repent.

If moral excellence is not present in us, we are one of the following things:

■ Not a Christian

■ A Christian who has failed to grow in the knowledge of God

■ A Christian who has forgotten God's precious promises

■ A Christian who is in rebellion and not submitting to the Spirit

■ A Christian who suffers from spiritual laziness

But moral excellence is possible when we trust in the finished work of Christ, surrender to the control of the Holy Spirit, and live in awareness of our need of God's grace to finish the race well.

Peter now tells us that to faith and goodness, we must add knowledge (2 Peter **1:5**). This is not the knowledge of God which leads to salvation (like the "knowledge" in **verses 2-3**, where a different Greek word is used). Rather, it refers to "the wisdom and discernment which the Christian needs for a virtuous life and which is progressively acquired" (Peter H. Davids, *The Letters of 2 Peter and Jude*, p 179). This kind of knowledge is related to our sanctification. It is a practical knowledge, the ability to manage life successfully. This type of knowledge does not grow naturally; it is the fruit of living in God's will. For this reason, as Gene L. Green counsels us in his commentary, "You must never separate the heart from the mind, character and knowledge" (quoted in Wiersbe, *2 Peter*, p 438).

> This is a practical knowledge, the ability to manage life successfully.

In this section of the letter, Peter is guiding us step by step. We must never stop climbing the ladder of growth—which is why Peter next tells us, "To knowledge, [add] self-control" (**v 6**). This means having control over ourselves or our impulses.

Throughout history the importance of self-control has been recognized by both believers and unbelievers alike. Aristotle, a Greek philosopher who lived four centuries before Christ, wrote, "The unrestrained man does things that he knows to be evil, under the influence of passion, whereas the self-restrained man, knowing that his desires are evil, refuses to follow them on principle" (quoted in Wiersbe, *2 Peter*, p 438).

But it should be clear to us that self-control is a **fruit of the Spirit**; it does not come purely as a result of human effort. In order to have self-control, we must be filled with the Spirit. (When we speak about being filled with the Spirit, we are referring to being under his control. The Spirit never has more or less power in us. Rather, he decides whether to manifest himself to a greater or lesser degree, depending on our degree of obedience.)

At this point Peter's ladder of virtue looks like this: Faith + goodness + knowledge + self-control. But this is still too short for him. It is not enough yet to help us run the race without stumbling. Therefore, he next adds "perseverance" to the list (**v 6**). Other translations render this word "patience." In his commentary on the letter to the Ephesians, William Barclay tells us that patience "bears insults and injury without bitterness and without complaint. It is the spirit that can suffer unpleasant people with graciousness, and fools without irritation" (*The Letters to the Galatians and Ephesians*, p 160).

In order for us to have an idea of the meaning of this word, we must understand that it is a term which often refers to God, who has been patient with humanity ever since the **fall**. In his letters, Paul calls us to be as patient with others as God has been with us (Colossians 3:12-13; Ephesians 4:2); this is a great challenge. Such patience means enduring and being able to stand firm under pressure without giving up our faith. Usually, patience is the fruit of having gone through tribulation (Romans 5:3-5).

We have three more steps to add to the ladder. The next one is godliness (2 Peter **1:6**). This refers to a lifestyle that...

- imitates Christ.

- makes every effort (to use Peter's language in **verse 5**) to do God's will.

- has the correct attitude and disposition toward God and others.

But the ladder of virtues does not end here. Now Peter adds "mutual affection." This refers to the concerns that we have for our brothers and sisters, whether they are of our biological or faith family. Jesus' disciples often did not possess this virtue, as is evident by the contentious arguments that frequently arose among them! Being contentious is typical of a prideful person, and pride will not allow us to finish well. In fact, Scripture says that pride comes before a fall (Proverbs 16:18). Instead, we must treat one another with humility and affection.

As if these seven characteristics were not enough, finally Peter adds love to the list: *agape*, sacrificial love. This is the love that...

- seeks the highest good in the other person.

- refuses to take advantage of the other person.

- loves unconditionally, keeping no record of offense.

- loves despite insult or injury.

This does not mean that *agape* love does not get hurt; but rather, when it is hurt, it can withstand pain for the benefit of others. This is the kind of love that brought Christ to the cross; it prefers to endure hurt before hurting others. Someone who loves in this way has one solitary interest: to give of themselves for the benefit of others. Those who show *agape* love do not find satisfaction in what they can receive but in what they can give. This is the love that not only has compassion for a neighbor but also sheds tears over the sins of others, just as Christ did on his way to Jerusalem (Luke 19:41).

What is Peter's interest in our developing these qualities? He provides the answer in 2 Peter **1:8**: "If you possess these qualities in increasing measure, they will keep you from being ineffective and unproductive in your knowledge of our Lord Jesus Christ." These virtues, in different degrees, should be part of each of our lives as Christians if we want to reflect God's character and be used by him. Otherwise, we will look like a fruitless and half-withered tree. A fruitless Christian usually has a lifestyle characterized by the worries and pleasures of this world. Remember when Jesus walked past a fig tree and cursed it for bearing no fruit (Matthew 21:18-19)? The fig tree represented Israel. Jesus' curse allows us to see that he would soon bring judgment on the nation for being fruitless. But we, too, should take that warning to heart. An idle Christian who does not bear fruit cannot finish well; he or she does not have what it takes to reach the end.

Peter does not expect us to be perfect Christians. He tells us that we must possess these qualities "in increasing measure"—that is, we must grow in each one. A new Christian who has very little self-control, for example, is not necessarily fruitless. What matters is that he or she is growing in that area. The growth may be gradual, but if that Christian is "making every effort" to know Christ and to represent him well, he or she will certainly bear fruit.

Don't Become Fruitless

Nevertheless, we must hear this as a warning. What is the implication for the believer who is uninterested in growing in Christ-likeness? Peter answers this question, too: "But whoever does not have [these qualities] is nearsighted and blind, forgetting that they have been cleansed from their past sins" (2 Peter **1:9**).

When Christians fail to exhibit Christ's character, we are forgetting that when we were born again, we were cleansed from the sins of our previous life. We have forgotten what Christ did for us. For this reason, Peter refers to such Christians as being blind or nearsighted.

They are shutting their eyes to Christ's light and his work. Without realizing it, they have given their will over to Satan's dominion.

Fruitless and idle Christians are the ones who end up falling away because they have paid attention to all kinds of false teachers. Such weak faith is fertile ground for the seeds of deception to grow quickly. By contrast, remembering what Christ did for us through his life, death, and resurrection produces gratitude, which is a powerful motivator for obedience. Why would you go back to your old life if you have a clear view of all that Christ is, and all he has gained for you?

Peter finishes this part of his letter by giving us the following recommendation: "Therefore, my brothers and sisters, make every effort to confirm your calling and election. For if you do these things, you will never stumble, and you will receive a rich welcome into the eternal kingdom of our Lord and Savior Jesus Christ" (**v 10-11**).

The key here, in light of everything we have said, is found in **verse 10**: "For if you do these things, *you will never stumble*" (emphasis added). If there ever was anyone who could talk about stumbling blocks and how to avoid them, it was the apostle Peter: yes, impulsive Peter…

- who spoke out of place,

- who thought of himself as more capable than the rest of the apostles,

- who denied and disowned his Lord.

Peter experienced these things, and he did not want you and me to have to experience them as well.

These verses are a warning to us that it is possible to become so cold in our faith that we become fruitless, returning to a lifestyle typical of those who have not believed. Peter is urging us to repent while there is still time. If we turn from sin and seek the qualities on his ladder of virtue, we will "confirm [our] calling and election" (**v 10**)—proving that we have indeed been saved and that the Spirit of the Lord is within us. And if that is so, then we will one day receive a "rich welcome" (**v 11**) before the eternal throne of God.

Questions for reflection

1. List the things God has provided for you to help you live as a Christian. What are some ways you can use those things?

2. What does it look like to be effective and productive in your knowledge of our Lord Jesus Christ (instead of ineffective and unproductive, v 8)?

3. Meditate on where you are regarding the virtues mentioned by Peter in v 5-7. What are some possible areas for growth?

2. REMEMBER WHAT YOU'VE LEARNED

In his book *Finishing Strong*, Steve Farrar tells the story of a conversation that a young man finishing college had with his future father-in-law, Dr. John Beck, after supper (p 15-16). Dr. Beck was an experienced minister, and he shared with his future son-in-law some lessons that he had learned over the years. He told the young man that, in his experience, "Just about one out of ten who start out in full-time service for the Lord at 21 are still on track by the age of 65." That was shocking to the young man. He went home, took his Bible, and on a blank page wrote the names of 24 young men he knew who were burning with passion for the Lord. He later related that by the time he reached 53 years of age, there were only three names that he hadn't had to cross out. That is one out of eight—very close to the one out of ten he had heard from his father-in-law. And these men had not even reached the age mentioned by Dr. Beck. What a sad reality!

Peter and Jude were aware that in the Christian life, what matters most is not how we start but how we go on. This is extremely important in this generation, which does not even like the word "sin." We prefer to think of ourselves as basically good; but we need to take seriously the possibility of going astray. I want to make the case about this possibility as strongly as possible, so that we can better understand the intensity of the words of the letters we are studying. Both Peter and Jude were distressed, burdened, and, on occasion, even angry with the way certain impostors were infiltrating the church.

Peter's Last Words

The reason why Peter was so concerned about how his readers would fare in the future was that he knew he himself did not have long left to live. "I know that I will soon put [my body] aside, as our Lord Jesus Christ has made clear to me" (2 Peter **1:14**). In some way, the Lord had revealed to Peter that after writing this letter he would soon be departing this life. This sounds very similar to Paul's words when he wrote to Timothy in his second letter: "For I am already being poured out like a drink offering, and the time for my departure is near" (2 Timothy 4:6). That letter has been called Paul's testament. Similarly, Peter's second letter can be seen as his testament or will. He wrote this letter of warning to his fellow believers in light of his imminent death. The final words of a well-respected person carry enormous weight, and Peter's words are no exception.

Some 1st-century wills have survived, and it is interesting to see the similarities between them and 2 Peter. Wills in Peter's day had the following things in common (as Douglas J. Moo points out in his commentary, *2 Peter, Jude,* p 64):

- The speaker knows (sometimes because of a prophecy) that he is about to die.

- The speaker gathers around him his followers or a similar audience.

- The speaker often impresses upon his audience the need for them to remember his teachings and example.

- The speaker makes predictions of the future.

- The speaker gives moral exhortations.

Peter does something very similar in this letter:

- He announces his departure.

- He directs the letter to his followers.

- He predicts a few things about the future.

- He gives some powerful exhortations for living a life of piety.

Peter writes with urgency. It is this we need to have in mind as we study the way the apostle sought to help his disciples not just to finish but to finish strong, for the glory of their Savior.

Some do not seem to care much about how they run the Christian race, as long as they finish in heaven. This attitude represents a low view of their salvation, their Lord, his cause, his glory, and his family on earth. We must live in reverence of God (1 Peter 1:17). It is this that will bring glory to him, by transforming us and making the gospel attractive to others.

Part of our problem, when we stray from the path, is that we forget or even ignore many of the truths we learned, practiced, taught, and even preached in the past. Unfortunately, with the passing of time, the truth of the Bible, its wonderful stories, its great heroes, and its awesome doctrinal teachings lose their novelty, and the things of the world begin to shine brighter. By not being careful, little by little, we find himself away from the Lord. Attending church or Bible study can convince us that our faith has not grown cold. Therefore, without realizing it, we learn to be content with living without the manifest presence of God in our life. The result is that some become so weakened by sin and by Satan that they fall away altogether.

The Call to Remember

The apostle Peter has already begun to help his readers to see the importance of recalling what they have learned (2 Peter 1:4, 9). Evidently, Peter knows from experience that many have drifted away from the faith after being a Christian for some time. They have lost the passion they once had for Jesus and the precious teachings of the gospel with all its implications. They have not been careful to keep as a priority that which was once of utmost importance.

Notice how Peter interacts with his readers: "So I will always remind you of these things, even though you know them and are firmly established in the truth you now have" (**v 12**). Their teacher is not going to tell them anything they do not already know. In fact, these believers know gospel truths so well that Peter considers them "firmly established in the truth." However, before Peter dies, he feels compelled to remind them, knowing that if they forget, their amnesia will make them stumble.

Peter seems almost obsessive about his readers' need to remember. He is determined to remind them of God's word...

- always (**v 12**).

- as long as he lives (**v 13**).

- by making every effort (**v 15**).

- even after his departure (presumably by leaving his instructions in writing, **v 15**).

It is not just here: we will see the same call to remember in 3:1-2. In a letter consisting of only three chapters, Peter points out to his readers the importance of *remembering* five times—and all to keep them from stumbling.

I do not think that many believers today are keenly aware of how crucial it is to remember, and how destructive it is to forget, the teachings of the Lord. The following passage was preached by Moses after 40 years of wandering in the desert, just weeks or days before crossing the Jordan river. It serves as a good illustration of what I am trying to say:

"Only be careful, and watch yourselves closely so that *you do not forget* the things your eyes have seen or let them fade from your heart as long as you live. Teach them to your children and to their children after them."

(Deuteronomy 4:9, emphasis added)

I like the expression "or let them fade from your heart" because this is usually the way it happens with us. After a certain amount of time has passed since our conversation, whatever we thought was great about the Lord and his ways becomes ordinary or routine. And what is ordinary is soon out of our memory. The author of the book of Proverbs is emphatic when he warns us in the name of the Lord:

"Get wisdom, get understanding; *do not forget* my words or turn away from them." (Proverbs 4:5, emphasis added)

Remembering on Time

It is not just the Lord's teachings we must keep in mind; it is also important to remember all that he has done. Reflecting on the way he has treated others will help us be clear about how he is likely to treat us. When we review the Old Testament, we may wonder why certain events were narrated with such detail and, at times, repeated in more than one book. Paul provides the answer in his first letter to the Corinthians: "These things happened to them as examples and were written down as warnings for us, on whom the culmination of the ages has come" (1 Corinthians 10:11). Others have lived through these events; it is our responsibility to read about, meditate on, and remember them. This is so that we may avoid the consequences others had to endure as part of the discipline and judgment of God.

Forgetting is the beginning of disobedience, just as the fear of the Lord is the beginning of wisdom. When we forget, we stop fearing God and, naturally, we stop fearing sin.

We forget the word → We stop fearing God → We stop fearing sin → We start living for the world and like the world → We fall away from the faith.

As I learned in elementary school, "To know is to remember on time." Remembering God's word on time may be the most effective way to prevent oneself from stumbling. This is how the psalmist expresses it: "I have hidden your word in my heart that I might not sin against you" (Psalm 119:11).

In the Gospels, we find Christ encouraging his disciples about the coming of the Holy Spirit as he approaches his own imminent departure. One vital role of the Spirit of God is precisely to remind the believer about the things he should never forget. In John 14:26 we read, "But the Advocate, the Holy Spirit, whom the Father will send in my name, *will teach you* all things and *will remind you* of everything I have said to you" (emphasis added). Jesus knew our great tendency to forget as we live under the constant pressure of the world, being attracted to, and sometimes even seduced by, the glamor of things which are temporal, earthly, and worldly. If forgetting was easy back then, it may be even easier today—in a world filled with temptations and new, creative ways of sinning that, thanks to the internet, are accessible, affordable, and anonymous.

> Jesus knew our great tendency to forget.

The 20th-century German pastor and theologian Dietrich Bonhoeffer observed that when lust takes control, "at this moment God ... loses all reality ... Satan does not fill us with hatred of God, but *with forgetfulness of God*" (quoted in R. Kent Hughes, *Disciplines of a Godly Man,* p 25). Satan uses our passions to cause us to forget—in the midst of our sinning—that there is a God who sees and judges everything. Would you have committed that sin yesterday if Christ had been present with you? In truth, he was; you just did not see him.

Don't fool yourself. The important thing is not that we hide our sins from other people. We will not be judged by people but by the Son of God (John 5:22), who is all-knowing. "Nothing in all creation is hidden from God's sight. Everything is uncovered and laid bare before the eyes of him to whom we must give account" (Hebrews 4:13).

So, Peter counsels us to remember. It is when we remain "firmly established in the truth" (2 Peter **1:12**) that we will keep from sinning and live in a way that honors our Lord and Savior.

Questions for reflection

1. When you listen to a sermon or read the Bible or a Christian book, do you make a significant effort to remember what you have heard or read? What hinders that desire or effort?

2. Is it your habit to put into practice what you learn? If no, why not? If yes, do you follow certain steps that you can share with others?

3. Do you agree with the statement made by Dietrich Bonhoeffer regarding our tendency to forget God when we are about to sin (whether the sin is lust or something else)?

PART TWO

The Source of Peter's Teaching

After teaching the need to retain or remember what has been learned, Peter goes on to explain the source of his teachings, in contrast with the origin of the teachings coming from the false prophets.

From **verse 16** onward, Peter reveals how he learned about the future coming of the Lord in power—which is the doctrine being denied by the false teachers. It seems that some were trying to undermine the apostolic authority of what he had taught his followers: "For we did not follow cleverly devised stories when we told you about the coming of our Lord Jesus Christ in power, but we were eyewitnesses of his majesty" (**v 16**). Peter lets them know that, unlike those who are trying to deceive the true disciples, his teachings are not the invention of his own imagination. Rather, he speaks as an eyewitness to events surrounding Jesus Christ, his Lord and Master.

Some of these experiences marked Peter in such a powerful way that when he and John were freed from prison and were forbidden to speak again about Christ, they responded by proclaiming, "As for us, we cannot help speaking about what we have seen and heard" (Acts 4:20). Only people who had been eyewitnesses could have been so marked and transformed. And only those who had been eyewitnesses could testify so accurately.

- Talking about something that others have related to you is not the same as talking about something that you have witnessed.

- Talking about something that you have read is not the same as talking about something through which you have lived.

- Talking about something that you know in your mind is not the same as talking about something that has transformed your life.

Peter is referring to one experience in particular: "We were eyewitnesses of his majesty" (2 Peter **1:16**). This is an allusion to what Peter, along with John and James, observed and heard at the Mount of

Transfiguration. "He [Christ] received honor and glory from God the Father when the voice came to him from the Majestic Glory, saying, 'This is my Son, whom I love; with him I am well pleased.' We ourselves heard this voice that came from heaven when we were with him on the sacred mountain" (**v 17-18**).

On that day, Moses and Elijah appeared and accompanied the Lord Jesus while the glory of God descended upon him, transfiguring him so that "his face shone like the sun, and his clothes became as white as the light" (Matthew 17:2). Matthew, like Peter, describes in his Gospel how the voice of God the Father was heard from heaven (17:5).

John's Gospel refers to the same experience: "We have seen his glory" (John 1:14). In Greek, the word for "see" used here is *theaomai*, which means to "look closely at" and not simply to glance at something. When Peter writes that he and others were "eyewitnesses" of Christ's glory, he is emphasizing the same thing: letting us know that they did not simply *see* some impressive events but that they had ample time to contemplate, behold, and meditate on them.

> In order to be good witnesses, we need to be good observers.

We too are witnesses of Christ—witnesses of all that he has done, even though we were not present during his earthly life. In order to be good witnesses, we need to be good observers. We need to contemplate with great attentiveness, because deliberate contemplation of and meditation on the facts not only leaves an indelible mark on our memory but also transforms us. This transformation is what allows us to tell the gospel story in the most passionate way.

All that Peter lived through gave him authority to speak and write about these revelations—by contrast with the false teachers, who talked about things that they never saw or heard firsthand, and instead created myths and fables to deceive weak sheep.

Once we get to the next chapter of 2 Peter, we will see more clearly that these false teachers were mockers of the truth; in particular, they denied the future coming of Christ. But the reality is that their target was about more than just denying Christ's second coming. If Christ were not to return, then there would be no final judgment. And if this judgment were not to take place, then people could live in any way they desired. Perhaps these teachers thought, just as many do today, "God is love, and therefore, at the end of history, he will simply forgive all of us." But if this were the case, there would have been no need for the cross: no need for Jesus to bear our sin. The truth is that sin is serious and judgment is coming. Each of us will appear before the judgment seat of Christ (2 Corinthians 5:10). So we need Christ's blood to cover us and justify us. Peter knew that the consequences of not believing that truth are very grave. This is why he underlined his own authority as against that of the false teachers.

The Authority of What Has Been Revealed

Next, Peter appeals to the authority of God's revelation. Since Peter is refuting the false teaching of those who are influencing the church in the wrong direction, it is only natural that he would anchor the truth on the One who is the source of that revelation: God.

Peter appeals to the authority of the Scriptures of the Old Testament, made known to God's people through Moses, Elijah, and other chosen prophets. This explains what follows in 2 Peter **1:19**: "We also have the prophetic message as something completely reliable."

Peter was an eyewitness of the miracles of Jesus. He walked on the water with him; he saw Christ transfigured; he saw the crucified and then resurrected Christ. But despite all of this, he seems to be saying that the written word of God in the Old Testament is more reliable than his own experiences.

The same is true of our own knowledge, understanding, and experiences. In our day the individual's viewpoint is often thought of as the most important source of truth. This is seen in our spiritual lives when we base our understanding of God only on our own experiences instead of on the Bible. But the word of the Lord reigns supreme—it is far more trustworthy than we are.

Notice how clearly Peter states this truth: "We also have the prophetic message as something completely reliable, and you will do well to pay attention to it" (**v 19**). Christ said something similar to **Thomas**: "Because you have seen me, you have believed; blessed are those who have not seen and yet have believed" (John 20:29). For Thomas, seeing was believing. Jesus was trying to teach his disciples that many had believed not on the basis of their own individual experiences but based on the word of God they had heard or read.

In the second part of **verse 19**, Peter compares the prophetic message to "a light shining in a dark place, until the day dawns and the morning star rises in your hearts." In other words, the prophetic message is a light that shines in the midst of sin until a transformation takes place in the heart. A person who is dominated by sin is a person in darkness. This is why Peter elsewhere speaks of us as having been brought from darkness into God's wonderful light (1 Peter 2:9). The apostle John uses a similar metaphor to describe the sinful opposition of the world to Christ and the certainty of Christ's triumph: "The light shines in the darkness, and the darkness has not overcome it" (John 1:5). It is the light of revelation that shines into the darkness of sin and restores us to repentance. Today, the same light shines through the faithful preaching of God's word.

A traveler without a light on a moonless night in the middle of the desert is completely lost. Likewise, without the light of the word, we would be lost. In his commentary on 1 and 2 Peter and Jude, David Helm narrates a story that shows the need for a "light" in order to finish well (*1 & 2 Peter and Jude,* p 215-216). I have adapted it here:

During the Second World War, six pilots took off during the night from an aircraft carrier. But upon their return, they could not find where the carrier was supposed to be. There were no lights on board: a blackout had been ordered due to the presence of enemy submarines in the area. So, the pilots could not see their location. One of the pilots communicated with the carrier by radio and asked to be given some light so he could land. The reply came: "Negative. We cannot give you any light at this moment. A black-out has been ordered." Moments later a second pilot repeated the request. "Negative. The blackout is still in effect." A third pilot—who had very little fuel—said, "Can't you at least give us one light so that we can land?" At this point, the radio operator was ordered to discontinue all contact. As a result, six pilots lost their lives in the darkness of the Atlantic waters.

You and I are not quite in the same situation as the pilots in the story. We do have the light we need to land: the testimony of God's word. But if we forget what we have learned, or we simply ignore it, we have essentially turned off that light—and our plane will inevitably crash. David Helm adds this challenge: "Many people today refuse to submit their lives and behavior to Jesus, on the charge they have not been given enough light to land. Until they see something or hear something or feel something, they simply will not believe they are ultimately going to be accountable to Someone for anything."

How Scripture Came About

Before the end of this first chapter, Peter declares a monumental truth necessary for all generations regarding the trustworthiness of the word of God:

> "Above all, you must understand that no prophecy of Scripture came about by the prophet's own interpretation of things. For prophecy never had its origin in the human will, but prophets, though human, spoke from God as they were carried along by the Holy Spirit." (2 Peter **1:20-21**)

This is a rich passage! We can learn several lessons from it.

First of all, the prophets of God in the past did not observe events or history and then give their own interpretation of how they understood what they had experienced. Neither did they receive an idea from God and then attempt to interpret what God wanted them to say before finally writing it down. No! They only wrote what came to them—by the direct inspiration of the Spirit, and sometimes even by dictation: "Then the LORD reached out his hand and touched my mouth and said to me, 'I have put my words in your mouth'" (Jeremiah 1:9).

Others have thought that the meaning of this passage in 2 Peter is that the Scriptures were not given to us to be interpreted in a personal way, each of us assigning to them the meaning we want. While that is true, it seems more consistent with the context to think that what Peter meant was that when the prophets wrote, they did not impose their own personal interpretation upon the Scriptures.

The second teaching from this passage is the understanding that no prophecy or teaching of the word ever came to the prophets of God primarily as a consequence of human desires, intentions, ideas, or initiatives. 2 Peter **1:21** denies that possibility: "Prophecy never had its origin in the human will." True prophets were not having personal dreams to which they would later lend their own interpretation. Humans are not the primary authors of the Scriptures. God is! They are the result of divine will.

Thirdly, when these men spoke, they did not do so independently. Rather, they did so by inspiration of the Holy Spirit and with such authority that it seemed as if God himself was the one speaking. As Augustine of Hippo (AD 354-430) would say, "When the Bible speaks, God speaks." This is why Paul writes to the Corinthians, "Unlike so many, we do not peddle the word of God for profit. On the contrary, in Christ we speak before God with sincerity, as those sent from God" (2 Corinthians 2:17).

The writers of the Scriptures often risked their lives preaching to an unbelieving world. Why? Because they were convinced that they had received their message from God. They had absolute confidence in the source and the power of the message they proclaimed. They knew perfectly well that they spoke on God's behalf. The preaching of a fallible word that came from themselves would call into question God's character, so they preached only what they knew came from him.

What we believe about the source of the Scriptures makes a monumental difference. In 1 Thessalonians, Paul speaks about the great testimony of the church at Thessalonica. In the next chapter, he mentions what made that possible: "When you received the word of God, which you heard from us, you accepted it not as a human word, but as it actually is, the word of God, which is indeed at work in you who believe" (1 Thessalonians 2:13). If we follow this logic, we can infer that frequently, when we disobey, it is ultimately down to having undermined the authority of the word. It is perhaps because we have already forgotten what we previously learned.

Questions for reflection

1. Why do you think false teachers often gain a large number of followers?

2. Believing that the Bible either is or is not the word of God greatly affects our obedience. In your own life, when you have disobeyed, what would you say was the number one reason?

3. What examples can you remember of how God's message has shone like a light in dark areas of your heart to transform you? What dark areas do you most long for him to transform now?

3. DANGER AND JUDGMENT

The second chapter of 2 Peter contains some of the most scalding rebukes against false teachers in the Bible.

In 2,000 years of church history, many have abandoned the faith; and many more will do the same before the second coming of Christ. Even in the most recent past, we have witnessed the fall of many very well-known church leaders. It is sad and painful to see those who once proclaimed the holiness of God commit treason against the God of their salvation. Some fall into immorality—even true believers— while others simply fall from the faith, showing that they never really belonged to the family of God (1 John 2:19). This is nothing new. In his second letter to Timothy, for example, Paul mentions eight people who compromised the faith or fell away:

- Phygelus and Hermogenes deserted Paul (2 Timothy 1:15).

- Hymenaeus and Philetus' teaching would "spread like gangrene" (2:17).

- Jannes and Jambres opposed Moses. (3:8).

- Demas loved this world and deserted Paul (4:10)

- Alexander "did me a great deal of harm" (4:14).

If these people had not been confronted, they would have preached the gospel in a distorted manner, causing great harm to the church.

As we run the Christian race along with others, we will notice that many will get tired and drop, while others will be seduced by the temptations of the world. We need to be prepared and be aware of how temptations work:

- We are only tempted by what we desire.

- The temptation that we face gets stronger as we use our imagination to create virtual realities.

- Once we are tempted, there is a tendency to rationalize giving in to it.

We must realize that temptations toward sin are not unrelated to misunderstandings about who God is. Many "runners" allow themselves to be deceived by false "truths" and are thereby led into sin. Having said that, we should keep in mind that the main spiritual problem is still the heart and its desires. The heart itself is "deceitful" (Jeremiah 17:9).

Origins of False Teachers

At the end of 2 Peter 1, Peter spoke of his own authority as a teacher and then affirmed the reliability of the prophecies of Scripture. His teaching is like that of the Old Testament prophets: it comes from God. Now he makes a similar comparison between false prophets who arose in the Old Testament and false teachers who are attacking the church in his own day. He wants us to consider where and how the false teachers arise: "But there were also false prophets among the people, just as there will be false teachers among you" (2 Peter **2:1**). False teachers may come from outside the church, but they also frequently come from within. This was the case with those Peter was dealing with—who had begun to wreak havoc among God's people.

False teachers who arise from within the church are the most dangerous because they look like any other brother or sister in the faith. The more pious false teachers appear to be, the more dangerous they are.

Insidious Influence

In the second part of **verse 1**, Peter begins to speak about how false teachers tend to work: "They will secretly introduce destructive heresies, even denying the sovereign Lord who bought them."

The history of the church has shown how clever these people can be. They introduce themselves in a secret or subtle manner, starting by agreeing with the truth. They preach it, teach it, and affirm it. Eventually, they introduce their false teachings *alongside* the truth. As a result, people hear both truth and false teaching at the same time. Finally, over time, these teachers begin to promote only false teachings without alluding to the truth at all. People end up forgetting what God is really like—which is the false teachers' ultimate goal. Instead, they elect to pursue the god of their own imagination, as the following text from Jeremiah allows us to see:

"I have heard what the prophets say who prophesy lies in my name. They say, 'I had a dream! I had a dream!' How long will this continue in the hearts of these lying prophets, who prophesy the delusions of their own minds? They think the dreams they tell one another will make my people forget my name, just as their ancestors forgot my name through Baal worship."

(Jeremiah 23:25-27)

These impostors are characterized by falsehood. Externally, they appear to be one thing when, in fact, internally, they are something completely different.

> The first false teacher was Satan himself.

The first false teacher in biblical history was Satan himself in the Garden of Eden. There, he began by questioning the word of God: "Did God really say, 'You must not eat from any tree in the garden'?" (Genesis 3:1). Then he proceeded to deny the word of God outright: "You will not certainly die" (3:4). Finally, he went on to distort God's word, claiming that instead of dying, Adam and Eve would become like God himself.

Notice the process: the word of God is questioned, then denied, and finally distorted.

Ever since, Satan has continued to deceive millions of people through human instruments. Here is how Paul describes this reality: "For such people are false apostles, deceitful workers, masquerading as apostles of Christ. And no wonder, for Satan himself masquerades as an angel of light. It is not surprising, then, if his servants also masquerade as servants of righteousness. Their end will be what their actions deserve" (2 Corinthians 11:13-15). Truly, our battle is not against flesh and blood, "but against the rulers, against the authorities, against the powers of this dark world and against the spiritual forces of evil in the heavenly realms" (Ephesians 6:12). Even though the real battle takes places in the heavenly places, it becomes visible through human instruments. As Warren Wiersbe writes, Satan "has false Christians … a false gospel … and even a false righteousness … One day he will present to the world a false Christ" (*The Bible Exposition Commentary*, p 446).

In summary:

- Satan disguises himself as an angel of light. He is the supreme representation of the world of darkness, but he presents himself as light; he is an imitator of God.

- His false apostles disguise themselves as Christ's apostles; they identify themselves not with the father of lies but with the embodiment of the truth.

- His servants masquerade as servants of righteousness. False prophets are evil people who strive to come across as pious people.

The goal of false teachers is to drive the disciples away from the truth. Their instrument of choice in carrying out their finest work is deceitfulness. Their preferred methodology, time and again, is to disguise themselves.

Once again, we can see this strategy employed in the Garden of Eden. Satan appeared as one of the animals of the field; he disguised himself as a serpent (disguise was his methodology). Today, he may appear as one of the pastors of the church of Christ or as a Sunday-school teacher or a regular member of the flock. Satan then proceeded to deceive Eve (deceitfulness was his instrument). Finally, he followed his well-thought-out plan until both Adam and Eve believed his lie and fell (driving them from the truth was his goal).

The false teachers Peter is referring to in this letter have promoted their heresies to the point of denying the "Lord who bought them" (2 Peter **2:1**). We might think that these people had been saved and later lost their salvation. However, this cannot be the case, since the doctrine of eternal security (the truth that once you are saved, you are always saved) is affirmed in multiple passages of Scripture (John 6:38-40; 10:28-30; Romans 8:31-39; Ephesians 1:13-14; Philippians 1:6). What Peter must mean is that these false teachers identified themselves as Christians; in the eyes of others and perhaps even in their own eyes, they had been bought by the Lord. But by living a lie and not accepting Jesus' lordship, they made it clear that they never really belonged to the family of God in the first place.

Serious Consequences

In time, all false teaching will result in devious behavior. As has been repeated so many times, ideas have consequences—which are sometimes severe and long-lasting. Peter had been commanded by Jesus to feed his sheep and to care for them (John 21:15-17). Consequently, he was concerned about the flock entrusted to him—and by now, he was even willing to give his life for those whom Christ had bought at a price. We can sense Peter's pastoral heart for the flock as he writes that "many will follow their depraved conduct and will bring the way of truth into disrepute" (2 Peter **2:2**).

False teachers sometimes speak with pious language, but their intentions and their actions are evil. The further their beliefs are from the truth, the more immoral their lifestyle is. In this one short sentence, Peter lets us see how corrupt these teachers are. He refers to their lifestyle as "their depraved conduct"—a bold and daring descrip- tion. Not only that; Peter also shows how significant their influence appears to be: "many will follow" not just their teaching but also their way of living. If no one paid attention to false teachers, their influence would not be felt. But the human heart has a tendency to follow the impulses of the flesh. These false teachers promoted sinful behavior; and this was successful, because that is how false disciples love to live.

But the impact of this sin was not just felt by individuals. By causing immature believers to sin, these false teachers were bringing "the way of truth into disrepute" (**v 2**).

Today, those who condemn preachers for calling out false teachers by name do not understand the impact that false teaching has on the gospel and, therefore, on the church. Peter should be our example in his unwillingness to allow these deceivers to teach a false gospel or even a false eschatology. Quite frequently, the world has accused Christians of not living up to their calling. Sinful behavior by Christians gives unbelievers a reason to mock us, our faith, and our God—and sinful behavior often arises from false teaching. This has been a major problem in church history since the 1st century. When Paul wrote the epistle to the Romans, one of his accusations against the legalistic Jews was precisely this: because of their sin and false teaching, "God's name is blasphemed" (Romans 2:24). This was not a small thing for Paul, and it should not be for any of us.

Unfortunately, millions of people around the world speak poorly about the Christian faith because of the poor testimony of the chil- dren of God. This was happening in the church of Rome, and now Peter says the same thing will happen to his readers if they continue to listen to the false teachers in their midst. When professing believers give way to a lifestyle full of sensuality and lies, it leads to shame being heaped upon the Christian faith.

Peter was dealing with charlatans who were not only sexually im- moral but also greedy: "In their greed these teachers will exploit you with fabricated stories" (2 Peter **2:3**). Sadly, people enjoy hearing fairy tales that satisfy their imagination and desires. This is the reason why false teachers prosper. It can be seen today in the prosperity gospel, which has only lined the pockets of its proponents while emptying the pockets of its followers.

During the ministry of the prophet Jeremiah, God said through him, "The prophets prophesy lies"; and as if that were not bad enough, God added, "and my people love it this way" (Jeremiah 5:31). People love lies because "everyone is a liar" (Psalm 116:11). How did false teachers exploit the people of their time? In the same way they do it today: "with fabricated stories." The tragedy of the human race began by believing the serpent's lie; then Abraham told lies about his wife; Isaac did the same thing; David lied about his sin with Bathsheba; and in the New Testament Ananias and Sapphira lied to Peter. Those are just a few examples!

But Christ hates lying lips because he is the truth. In fact, he told Pilate that he came to testify to the truth (John 18:37). He is the one we must turn to if we are to overcome false teaching.

Questions for reflection

1. What false teachings do you see in the church today? What happens when people believe those false teachings?

2. Do you think false teachings today tend to come more from inside the church or more from the culture around us? What examples could you give of both?

3. What does the phrase "the sovereign Lord who bought [you]" mean for you?

PART TWO

Judgment is Sure

False prophets are thieves of the truth. Once the truth is gone, there is nothing left of any value. The absence of the truth in a church is the sign that it's time to leave it. Exposing ourselves to doctrinal errors will have a harmful effect on us. Similarly, if the people to whom a pastor is preaching the truth are not willing to listen, it may be that the only option left for that pastor is to depart from that church. Paul did something similar when he departed from the Jews in Pisidian Antioch to go to Iconium (Acts 13:51).

Truth is non-negotiable. If we negotiate over the truth, we negotiate over the fate of our soul. If we walk in the truth, we walk with God. If we walk in lies, we walk with Satan. "What harmony is there between Christ and Belial?" (2 Corinthians 6:15). None! We must run from heresies and doctrinal errors.

At the end of 2 Peter **2:1**, Peter encourages us to do this by reminding us that false teachers will eventually bring "swift destruction upon themselves." Lies are destructive to the message of salvation and to the people of God. Therefore, although God in his mercy may delay his judgment, he will not remain silent permanently.

God "is patient with you, not wanting anyone to perish, but everyone to come to repentance" (3:9). God is slow to anger, but he is not a God without anger. Sin, especially intentional sin, makes him angry (Romans 1:18-120). God is filled with mercy, but mercy is not his only attribute. A God who is not angry at wrongdoing is like a judge who has no feeling against lawlessness—and who would want such a judge?

Things may go well for the false teachers, perhaps even for a long time. But the situation will not remain the same forever because God is not indifferent to the corruption of the truth. He has always vindicated the holiness of his name after his people have profaned it. So, Peter tells us, "Their condemnation has long been hanging over them, and their destruction has not been sleeping" (2 Peter **2:3**).

2 Peter 2 v 1-10a

Judgment will come, although perhaps neither at the time nor in the way that we may desire.

God's Judgments in the Past

To prove this point, Peter now provides three examples from the past of how God carried out his judgment on those who had sinned.

1. Angels Who Sinned

The first illustration comes from the angelic realm: "God did not spare angels when they sinned, but sent them to hell, putting them in chains of darkness to be held for judgment" (**v 4**).

God did not provide a plan of redemption for the angels. Instead, they were condemned forever. This may seem strange; after all, we don't often talk about God judging angels. But many scholars believe that Isaiah 14:12-15 and Ezekiel 28:2-10 allude to the fall of Satan, who began as an angelic being (see Douglas J. Moo, *The NIV Application Commentary*, Kindle loc. 2224). In addition, the text of Revelation 12:7-9 may indicate that when Satan fell, he rebelled along with a number of the heavenly hosts (see James M. Hamilton Jr., *Revelation*, p 247-8). In his first epistle Peter also makes mention of a number of angels who sinned in the days of Noah, who have been kept in dark prisons due to the magnitude of their transgression (1 Peter 3:19-20). These events related to the judgment of angelic beings clearly made a strong impression on Peter's mind—to the point that he mentions them in both of his epistles. Jude also does so in Jude v 6, as we will see later in this book.

What did these angels from Noah's days do? Genesis 6:2 describes a moment in time when the "sons of God" entered into union with the "daughters of man." Tradition holds that the term "sons of God" is a reference to fallen angels and that the "daughters of man" were human women. These angels may be the ones that Peter and Jude describe as being kept in eternal chains under gloomy darkness because of their sinfulness.

But regardless of who exactly these angels were and what they did, the point is that their actions were so wicked that God "sent them to hell, putting them in chains of darkness to be held for judgment" (2 Peter **2:4**). In Greek mythology, the terms "hell" and "chains of darkness" refer to the deepest and darkest places of the underworld (see Gundry, *Commentary on the New Testament*, p 960). Peter is helping us to understand that when God brings down his judgment, it can be extremely severe.

2. The Flood

The second example is the flood, which inundated the entire earth and all its "ungodly people" (**v 5**). Peter is seeking to illustrate both that our holy God is capable of taking extreme measures when dealing with sin and that he acts to save the righteous. God punished the entire world—but he also preserved Noah, along with seven others related to him: his wife, his three sons, and his sons' wives.

It took Noah 120 years to build the ark, and during this time he was a "preacher of righteousness." Yet no one paid attention to him—with the exception of his immediate family. "All the people on earth had corrupted their ways" (Genesis 6:12). Likewise, many today are living self-centered and immoral lives. The human heart does not change! That will continue until God exercises his judgment again. But Christ is like the ark that preserved Noah. In the midst of the perversion of our current age, God can preserve us—if we do not become like the world. Otherwise, our fate will be like the fate of the lawless.

3. Sodom and Gomorrah

The third illustration Peter uses to warn his readers is related to the condemnation of Sodom and Gomorrah. God burned these cities to ashes, making them "an example of what is going to happen to the ungodly" (2 Peter **2:6**). Peter is demonstrating once again that, in the fullness of time, God always judges the wicked—and always has done.

Like Noah, Lot is used as an example of a godly and righteous man who lived among wicked people and who was rescued when they were destroyed. This is interesting given that Lot's track record was very different to Noah's. Lot was Abraham's nephew, and he lived in Sodom (Genesis 14:12). This was a poor decision—Sodom was renowned as a city of immorality—and it had serious consequences. Lot did not live at peace; rather, he "was distressed by the depraved conduct of the lawless" (2 Peter **2:7**). Moreover, the text adds that Lot "was tormented in his righteous soul by the lawless deeds he saw and heard"

> Holiness reacts to sin—and it needs to stay away from sinfulness.

(**v 8**). Holiness reacts to the sin in ourselves, in others, and in society. But holiness needs to stay away from sinfulness, because ultimately the holy may become unholy—as Paul explains: "Do not be misled: 'Bad company corrupts good character'" (1 Corinthians 15:33). We can see this truth in the Genesis narrative. When the men demanded that Lot allow his three visitors (who were angelic beings) to come out so they could have sexual relations with them, Lot's answer was *not* the most righteous:

> "Look, I have two daughters who have never slept with a man. Let me bring them out to you, and you can do what you like with them." (Genesis 19:8)

Lot offered his two virgin daughters to be raped by these wicked men in order to protect his visitors. Never mind the customs of the time, which put a high value on the way you treated guests: this was not a godly answer.

Yet, even in Lot's case, God showed mercy. He rescued Lot from Sodom, which was destroyed as a result of its people's sexual perversion. Commentator J. Daryl Charles notes, "Although Noah and Lot are worlds apart in terms of their personal and ethical example, both are objects of God's redeeming and unmerited favor. Given the fact that Lot's character, based on the Genesis narrative, leaves much to be desired, the readers of 2 Peter can take courage" (*The Expositor Bible Commentary*, p 400). I would add, however, that this last comment does not mean that believers could or should take license to sin.

In his commentary on 2 Peter, David Helm makes the following observation regarding how we should respond to the story of Sodom and Gomorrah:

"What a powerful reminder for those of us who are trying to keep from falling. When we return to the enticements of the world, we are only demonstrating that we have no power over it. And when we begin to think that there will be no conse-quences for our private behavior, that God is love and only love, and that nothing bad will ever happen to us, we are in danger not only of self-deception but of becoming the recipi-ents of God's righteous wrath. Men, to you I speak more spe-cially: when you live in unrestrained material ease and indulge in every sexual freedom, you reduce your dignity to that of a moth drawn to the flame. And beneath the bright light of the immoral city, God's fiery judgment will come once again."

(*1 & 2 Peter and Jude*, p 228)

By appealing to the fact that God is love, many who profess to be Bible-believing Christians categorically deny the existence of hell or the possibility that God may discipline his own people, sometimes even severely. You may think that this denial is a new idea or a new teaching, but it is not. Peter provided three different examples from the past as he tried to convince the believers in his own day not to pay attention to the false teachers who denied the second coming of Christ and a future judgment. He concludes:

"If this is so, then the Lord knows how to rescue the godly from trials and to hold the unrighteous for punishment on the day of judgment. This is especially true of those who follow the cor-rupt desire of the flesh and despise authority." (2 Peter **2:9-10**)

Peter is reiterating what he has already illustrated. God rescued Noah and at the same time flooded the earth. He rescued Lot and at the same time punished the wicked in Sodom and Gomorrah. Peter is calling his readers to avoid making the same mistake that the people of those cities made. We must not be those who follow the instincts of the flesh; we must make sure that we do not rebel but submit to the authority of Jesus, who "knows how to rescue the godly from trials" (**v 9**).

Questions for reflection

1. Can you recall a time in your life when you were deceived in an area of doctrinal belief? What led to the deception? How did you discover your error?

2. Christ said, "My sheep listen to my voice … and they follow me" (John 10:27). However, his sheep also listen to other voices and sometimes even follow false teachers. Why is this? What helps us distinguish Christ's voice from others'?

3. In what regards are you tempted to "follow the corrupt desire of the flesh" or to despise the authority of your Savior (2 Peter 2:10)? What help do you need to overcome temptation?

4. HOW TO RECOGNIZE FALSE TEACHERS

False teachers have been around since the beginning of the biblical narrative. We already saw that the first false teacher was Satan himself. The classroom was the Garden of Eden, and the students were only two: Adam and Eve, who made a fatal decision that brought consequences to the human race for the rest of this world's history. Although they frequently appear pious, false teachers are deadly; their intention is destructive, and their teaching is from hell (1 Timothy 4:1). Our Lord warned us about them:

"Watch out for false prophets. They come to you in sheep's clothing, but inwardly they are ferocious wolves. By their fruit you will recognize them. Do people pick grapes from thornbushes, or figs from thistles? Likewise, every good tree bears good fruit, but a bad tree bears bad fruit. A good tree cannot bear bad fruit, and a bad tree cannot bear good fruit. Every tree that does not bear good fruit is cut down and thrown into the fire. Thus, by their fruit you will recognize them."

(Matthew 7:15-20)

According to our Lord Jesus Christ, false teachers…

- may look like any other sheep.

- usually have malicious hearts, like ferocious wolves.

- bear bad fruit even if they sound godly when speaking.

- will one day receive the judgment that is due them.

- are known or recognized by the fruit they bear.

False teachers are always inventing new ways of packaging the lies they teach. The exchange of the truth for a lie is the origin of idolatry. Once this exchange takes place, the next step is the worshiping of the creature instead of the Creator (Romans 1:25).

Today, false teachers abound around the world—and, as expected, they exhibit similar characteristics to those of the past. Their teaching is not based on the revealed word, but rather, on "new revelations" such as dreams and visions. Sometimes there is an overemphasis on the work of the Spirit, to the point of eclipsing the work of Christ. Since no one wants to be accused of contradicting the Holy Spirit, many who do not know the Bible well tend to accept these teachings, even when they are different from what we find in Scripture. But we must remember that the Spirit came to glorify the Son (John 16:14), and so no words that truly come from the Spirit could contradict the word that has already been revealed.

The Arrogance of False Teachers

The next section in 2 Peter 2 gives us an idea of how perverse false teachers can be. Peter now describes their character. He begins by mentioning their arrogance, which has reached such a degree that they dare to curse celestial beings, whose might is far superior to theirs.

"Bold and arrogant, they are not afraid to heap abuse on celestial beings; yet even angels, although they are stronger and more powerful, do not heap abuse on such beings when bringing judgment on them from the Lord." (2 Peter **2:10-11**)

Who are these celestial beings? Peter seems to be referring to angelic beings who have fallen (see Peter H. Davids, *The Letters of 2 Peter and Jude*, p 234-36). He has already mentioned angels who sinned, describing them as being "held for judgment" by God (v 4); here the celestial beings are also to be judged (**v 11**), and so it seems likely that the fallen angels and the celestial beings are one and the same.

Peter's point is that the arrogance of these false teachers is such that they believe they have the power and authority to do what even angels do not dare to do: to heap abuse on the celestial beings. We will find a very similar idea in Jude v 9, where the archangel Michael holds back from pronouncing judgment against the devil (a fallen angel) and instead prefers to have the Lord himself rebuke him. The angels of 2 Peter **2:11** are "stronger and more powerful" than the fallen celestial beings, and are able to bring God's judgment upon them; but it is God's judgment, not theirs, and so they do not dare to heap abuse on them. The false teachers, by contrast, think that they themselves have the authority not only to judge the celestial beings but to speak abusively of them.

I believe we have seen this behavior in the spiritual-warfare movement that has been so popular in the last 40 years. We have seen and heard a number of men and women mocking demons and even Satan, as they try to expel them from people who seem to be possessed. These "exorcists" claim to have the "gift of liberation." In the exercise of this "gift," they love to flaunt their own "authority."

This may be the kind of thing Peter is referring to in this passage. He calls these teachers "bold and arrogant." He also considers them insolent, irrational, and ignorant:

> "But these people blaspheme in matters they do not understand. They are like unreasoning animals, creatures of instinct, born only to be caught and destroyed, and like animals they too will perish. They will be paid back with harm for the harm they have done."

Peter compares them to irrational animals which are eventually captured and killed (**v 12-13**). In other words, God's judgment upon them will be severe. The apostle Paul writes to the Romans that the wrath of God is "revealed from heaven against all the godlessness and wickedness of people, who suppress the truth by their wickedness" (Romans 1:18). God is angry at the suppression of his truth; he is even more wrathful when lies are preached in his name. Imagine how much more provoked he is when those who dare to do such a thing are boastful and arrogant! We can rest assured that God will "not leave the guilty unpunished" (Numbers 14:18).

The Lifestyles of Arrogant Teachers

Next Peter proceeds to speak about the false teachers' immoral life-style. Here is what we read in 2 Peter **2:13**: "Their idea of pleasure is to carouse in broad daylight. They are blots and blemishes, reveling in their pleasures while they feast with you."

- They had no shame in showing their immoral behavior.

- Their lives were morally filthy.

- They were living in this way among the brothers of the church, eating with them as if nothing untoward was happening.

- Their consciences were numb, so that they found immorality a pleasure.

The New Living Translation (NLT) describes them in this very graphic way: "They love to indulge in evil pleasures in broad daylight. They are a disgrace and a stain among you. They delight in deception even as they eat with you in your fellowship meals."

Worst of all, they were "teachers" who moved among the church family looking like true Christians, while teaching lies to cover up their immorality. You have to wonder how they were tolerated among true believers!

These people ignored or disregarded the warning given to us in James 3:1: "Not many of you should become teachers, my fellow believers, because you know that we who teach will be judged more strictly."

They took advantage of the most vulnerable sheep, the weakest ones—perhaps those less spiritually or emotionally mature or perhaps those with some special condition that made them easy prey. The false teachers seduced these sheep in the same way the serpent seduced

Adam and Eve: they twisted the truth of God to the point of changing it altogether.

As if that were not enough, these people were guilty of adultery, even while teaching the word of God. So they were doubly guilty. "With eyes full of adultery, they never stop sinning" (2 Peter **2:14**). Their desire for sin was insatiable; it wasn't just that they sinned, but that sin *characterized* their lives. And "they seduce the unstable." Instability was their goal; they were heart-less; and they knew which prey to stalk. Rather than caring for the most vulnerable, they used them to satisfy their own appetites. Remember, these people had disciples and were respected as teachers. They knew God's word, but they used false teachings to cover up what they really were.

> The false teachers were like the serpent: they twisted the truth of God.

In our own days, too, we have witnessed immorality among a number of false teachers. This was true of false teachers in the time of the people of Israel, it was true of them in the time of the New Testament writings, and it is true of them to this day.

Additionally, they were greedy: "experts in greed—an accursed brood!" Simply put, they were well-trained in how to take money from people. No wonder that the clearest example of false teaching at the end of the 20th century and the beginning of this one has been the prosperity gospel: the idea that you will become rich if you pray in a certain way or give money to certain teachers. Many exponents of this teaching have lived extravagant lives and have ministered in a very arrogant way. They are "experts in greed."

Spiritual Warfare in Our Days

Since both 2 Peter and Jude deal so much with false teachers and the influence of the spirit world, it is important to understand what spiritual warfare is and is not.

At the cross Jesus defeated sin in our behalf; with his resurrection, he defeated death. In addition, Jesus triumphed over the "powers and authorities" [and] he made a public spectacle of them (Colossians 2:15). Therefore, our spiritual warfare is not a power encounter—Jesus has already won. It is, rather, a battle for the truth. Satan is the father of lies (John 8:44) and a master of deception.

The battle for the truth goes on in our minds (2 Corinthians 11:3; Romans 7:22-24), but the lies come to us in places like classrooms, movies, the internet, commercials and in many other ways. We fight the world and its influence. We also fight our own flesh. This conflict between the flesh and the Spirit is part of our spiritual warfare—so much so that Peter speaks about our "sinful desires, which *wage war* against your soul" (1 Peter 2:11, emphasis added). Finally, we fight the devil himself. There is no question that Satan has ways of exercising influence over us.

Demon possession is one extreme form of spiritual warfare. We should not allow our "modern minds" to reject the truth, revealed in God's word, that demons are real and can take possession of people. Those in mission fields where people are more involved in the occult are more familiar with this. But, as with other forms of spiritual warfare, it would be an error to assume in these cases that we are facing a "power encounter" when, in reality, we are facing a "truth vs lie encounter." What leads people into demon possession is worship of idols, which peddle lies—as Paul explains in Romans 1:25.

When Jesus faced the devil's temptations, he quoted the Scriptures three times to push the evil one back (Matthew 4:1-11)—fighting the devil's lies with truth. In the same way, Paul encourages us to "stand firm then, with the belt of *truth* buckled around your waist" (Ephesians 6:14, emphasis added) and to wield the "sword of the Spirit, which is the word of God" (v 17). The word is God's truth revealed to humanity. It is that word that was distorted in the garden and it is the same word that false teachers continue to distort. It is this word that is the key to our fight against the world, the flesh and the devil.

Questions for reflection

1. How can you recognize false teachers today? If there were false teaching in your church, what steps would you take to deal with it?

2. Can you think of any reason why God allows false teachers to infiltrate his church?

3. In what ways would you say you have experienced spiritual warfare? How has this chapter helped you develop a biblical attitude toward the devil?

PART TWO

Nothing New under the Sun

Solomon was right when he said, "What has been will be again, what has been done will be done again; there is nothing new under the sun" (Ecclesiastes 1:9). The sin committed by people in the Old Testament was committed again by different people in the New Testament and is being committed by still more people today. In 2 Peter **2:15-16**, Peter summarizes a very well-known story that took place hundreds of years before, as he seeks to explain how these false teachers are following the same path:

> "They have left the straight way and wandered off to follow the way of Balaam son of Bezer, who loved the wages of wickedness. But he was rebuked for his wrongdoing by a donkey—an animal without speech—who spoke with a human voice and restrained the prophet's madness."

The story of Balaam appears in Numbers 22 – 25. Balak was the king of the Moabites, and he was afraid of the Jews. Therefore, he called on Balaam, a prophet who was serving God at the time. Balaam knew the truth of God and God's will, but unfortunately, in time, he abandoned the path of righteousness.

One day, Balaam was offered a bribe from Balak, via some messengers, to curse Israel. He rejected this bribe. The king of the Moabites then sent him a larger offering, accompanied by a greater number of messengers—these ones more impressive-seeming than the first. At that point, although he had already been told by God not to go with the messengers, Balaam said he would think and pray about it. He ended up going with them on the road to see Balak.

Think for a moment. Is there anything to pray about regarding such a wicked action? Did Balaam really think that God would allow him to curse the Jews for a larger sum of money? Balaam had begun to flirt with wrongdoing and had started to rationalize his sin. By justifying our sin, we commit another sin.

In the account in Numbers, we see how God used Balaam's donkey to rebuke the prophet. Balaam had lost his mind when he went with Balak's messengers. This is why Peter says in 2 Peter **2:16** that Balaam's donkey rebuked "the prophet's madness." Unfortunately, madness is what the desire for money leads us into—and sin in general. Don't forget that the false teachers Peter is talking about were immoral and greedy. Lust and money have the same power to make us so irrational that we could be described as mad.

The Slippery Slope of Sin

The love of money can make us rationalize our sin. The same can be said of any desire of the flesh. We should keep in mind that…

- sin will take us beyond where we intended to go in the first place.

- sin will keep us away from God longer than we thought.

- sin will cost us more than we wanted to pay.

- we sin on our terms, but we will have to come back on God's.

- sin begets sin: with one sin we tend to cover another sin.

Balaam started by refusing the offer; then he asked for time to think and pray about it. About what? About accepting a bribe to curse God's people. God kept saying no. Perhaps Balaam was getting upset that God was not giving him the green light to make a profit. Listen to the psalmist: "When my heart was grieved and my spirit embittered, I was senseless and ignorant; I was a brute beast before you." Don't miss the way the author describes himself: "senseless;" "ignorant;" "a brute beast" (Psalm 73:21-22).

When Balaam asked for time to pray to see if God would allow him to take the bribe, at that moment his heart had begun to harden. He asked God if he could go to Balak with his messengers. God, in his permissive will, told him that he could. God was testing how far Balaam was willing to go in order to receive a bribe. On his way to meet the king of the Moabites, Balaam's donkey stopped because the angel of the Lord stood in the middle of the road, and the donkey veered out of the way. But again, the angel of the Lord stood in front of the donkey. This same thing happened three times (Numbers 22:21-31).

Balaam knew the path of righteousness, and yet he strayed. Therefore, he can be considered a true apostate. *The Evangelical Dictionary of Theology* defines apostasy as "a deliberate repudiation and abandonment of the faith that one has professed (Hebrews 3:12)." Balaam was someone who had a connection with God and was able to receive direct instructions from him. Yet he still turned away from the path of righteousness. Balaam's story is a perfect illustration of the problem of the false teachers that Peter is referring to. They were greedy, immoral men who loved money more than God; they knew the way of the truth, as we will see later, but they decided to leave it and renounce the faith.

A Threat to All Our Faith

God's indignation against false teachers is clearly demonstrated in Peter's words in this letter. Pride, greed, lust, deceitfulness and abuse of power have all been associated with them. When Peter shone his light on the false teachers of his time, that was the dirt he found. A deceitful heart can easily be enticed to follow the wrong path; our flesh will always enjoy the way of the world; but then we hate the slavery produced by following the desires of our flesh.

Perhaps you believe that this discussion about false teachers and their desires for money and immoral lifestyle has nothing to do with you because you are not a teacher of the word or a leader. But the stories gathered in the Bible were recorded for the instruction of us all. And all of us may experience the kind of attraction to money that these false teachers experienced. For some, the desire to make money can be all-consuming. For others, the idea of spending money may be distressing, causing us to continually search out ways to spend one dollar less—which can also become an obsession and therefore be debilitating.

We may think we would not be willing to violate our conscience for a certain amount of money. But we might consider it and may even pray for it, as Balaam did.

I am convinced that the clear teaching of the Bible is that nothing competes with God the way the love of money does. In the first place, we are told that "the love of money is a root of all kinds of evil" (1 Timothy 6:10). And secondly, when Jesus tried to show the supremacy of his lordship, he compared love for him with love of money:

"No one can serve two masters. Either you will hate the one and
love the other, or you will be devoted to the one and despise
the other. You cannot serve both God and money."

(Matthew 6:24)

Those who are still trying to serve two masters are the ones most likely to be allured by false teachers.

What pleasures are you seeking that call you away from the path of righteousness? You might not "carouse in broad daylight" as the false teachers did in Peter's time (2 Peter **2:13**). And yet perhaps you secretly indulge in pornography. Others are involved in adultery (**v 14**) but deny it again and again. For all of us there will be some particular pleasure which tempts us away from what is right.

God is always watching us and calling us back to the right path, but it is up to us to heed his voice. We must remember that pleasure is fleeting, temporary, and transient; but the consequences of sin are long-lasting. God cannot be mocked (Galatians 6:7).

One more observation: the more we walk in darkness, the easier it is to fall prey to false teachers. Only the light of Christ can penetrate dark minds and hearts. Christ said, "I am the light of the world" (John 8:12)—of a world that lies in darkness. It is my desire and prayer that the darkness around us will always drive us to the light.

False Teachers Are Dead

Frequently, when the Bible speaks about people being dead or alive, it is referring not to physical death or life but to one's spiritual state. For example, Ephesians 2:1 says, "As for you, you were dead in your transgressions and sins." In that sense, we can easily say that false teachers are dead, which is why Peter speaks about them in these terms: "These people are springs without water and mists driven by a storm. Blackest darkness is reserved for them" (2 Peter **2:17**). If their followers were to "drink" from them in the same way that true disciples drink of Jesus, they would die thirsty. False teachers have no living water, and a spring without water is not a spring at all. It is just a furrow in the ground, which is completely useless. Or the false teachers are like a mist or fog that is quickly blown away by the wind of a storm. These are those for whom darkness is reserved.

> False teachers have no living water, and a spring without water is not a spring at all.

Peter seems to have endless ways of describing these wicked teachers! They are arrogant and boastful, and yet their words are empty and full of deceitfulness. They go after new converts, who lack knowledge and who perhaps are still struggling with recent sin in their lives. This is the way Peter explains it: "by appealing to the lustful desires of the flesh, they entice people who are just escaping from those who live in error" (**v 18**). Once we are born again, we start a process of sanctification; this may be harder at the beginning, especially for those who have spent a long time in the practice of addictive sin patterns. Those who are "just escaping" may be particularly vulnerable to the temptation to go back.

Obviously, false teachers need a good strategy; so, they promise their followers that they will bring them to freedom (**v 19**). So today, the teachers of the prosperity gospel promise their disciples that they will bring them out of financial difficulty if they will simply give God a certain amount of money, which, in due time, God will multiply in great measure. But there is a problem with that promise. It is not biblical. This false freedom is not the true freedom that God offers. The false teachers—both Peter's and ours—offer this heresy while "they themselves are slaves of depravity—for 'people are slaves to whatever has mastered them'" (**v 19**). False teachers do not have the ability to make anyone free. Rather, "if the Son sets you free, you will be free indeed" (John 8:36).

We have true freedom in Christ. All the more reason not to play with sin and come back under its mastery. Sin...

- deceives.

- clouds our understanding.

- makes us believe things that we would otherwise never believe.

- makes us dream of the impossible.

- controls our lives, our hearts, and our minds to the point of not letting us rest. That is why we become slaves.

Peter closes this section of the text with very a serious warning:

"If they have escaped the corruption of the world by knowing our Lord and Savior Jesus Christ and are again entangled in it and are overcome, they are worse off at the end than they were at the beginning. It would have been better for them not to have known the way of righteousness, than to have known it and then to turn their backs on the sacred command that was passed on to them." (2 Peter **2:20-21**)

Knowing the truth only to live in violation of it is worse than living in ignorance of it. This is what Peter is saying. The more we know, the more responsibility we have. I don't think most of us have given enough consideration to what it means to know the truth. We are accountable to the truth whether we know it or not, but our level of accountability and future judgment increases with our knowledge of revealed truth.

Jesus, too, spoke about this, albeit in a different context:

"From everyone who has been given much, much will be demanded; and from the one who has been entrusted with much, much more will be asked." (Luke 12:48)

God wants us to know the truth, because the truth…

- sets us free,

- allows us to have communion with God,

- brings peace to our heart,

- prevents us from becoming an idolater, and…

- produces joy in us.

But knowing the truth and then turning our back on it brings terrible consequences.

By way of illustration, Peter concludes the chapter with two vividly unpleasant images: "Of them the proverbs are true: 'A dog returns to its vomit,' and, 'A sow that is washed returns to her wallowing in the mud' (2 Peter **2:22**).

Imagine a dog which vomits up something that poisoned it, and then goes back to eat it once again. This is a good comparison with what sin does. We come to Christ and confess to him the sins that have all but ruined our lives. Christ cleanses us and forgives us as we give our lives to him. We start to make progress in our lives—then, suddenly, we decide to go back and start sinning all over again. The consequences are certain to be worse because now we are compromising the gospel. We are trampling over Jesus' blood and behaving like pagans, but under the name of Jesus.

We must heed the author of the book of Hebrews, who tells us, "But encourage one another daily, as long as it is called 'Today,' so that none of you may be hardened by sin's deceitfulness" (Hebrews 3:13). In Christ there is an opportunity every day—even every hour—to return to his ways and be cleansed and forgiven once again.

Questions for reflection

1. Why is it so hard to stop sinning once you have started on the slippery slope?

2. Do you think Balaam was a true prophet of God at some point, or was he always an impostor? What biblical evidence supports your view?

3. Toward the end of this chapter, I mentioned several things that sin is capable of doing in us. How have you seen that influence in your own life? What helps you to fight sin?

5. THE LORD WILL RETURN

The second coming of Christ was a frequent topic of conversation in the 1970s during the Jesus Movement in the United States, the ripple effects of which were felt even in Latin America, where my wife and I reside. It seemed that everyone was talking about Christ's return. However, over the last four decades the enthusiasm has slowly disappeared. Today we rarely hear an entire sermon on the second coming, and I cannot recall the last time I saw an announcement for a conference on eschatology (teaching about the end times). If we do dare to mention the topic in our day, it is very likely that we'll be seen as pessimists, since the day of the Lord involves a final judgment for those who have not believed. But it is supposed to be a day of celebration for the believers.

When authors of the Bible mention that a future judgment is coming, they usually do so for two distinct reasons:

1. *To encourage believers to wait patiently in a world of injustice.* In this world it can often seem as if it doesn't matter how we live our lives; there are no consequences for acting unjustly, and the wicked prosper. This has always been the case. It was articulated in this way in Old Testament times: "There is something else meaningless that occurs on earth: the righteous who get what the wicked deserve, and the wicked who get what the righteous deserve. This too, I say, is meaningless" (Ecclesiastes 8:14). How will anyone be motivated to live morally in a world that seems indifferent to the way we live? In 2 Peter 3, Peter will remind us that the way we live this side of glory *does* matter in light

of eternity. Judgment is coming, when the righteous will receive their reward and the wicked their due punishment.

2. *To awaken the sinner to the reality of the coming judgment.* Peter talks about the second coming not just for the sake of theological clarity but as a strong encouragement to live morally. As we'll see, these two ideas come together in 2 Peter 3:11: "Since everything will be destroyed in this way, what kind of people ought you to be? You ought to live holy and godly lives."

In our day, in one way or another, I think believers are too comfortable in this world; that is why we are not excited about the coming of the next one. Some even hope that Christ's return will be delayed so that they can get married, while others hope to have grandchildren before Christ comes back. I have heard those sentiments more frequently than I wish. When I hear such comments, I pause and wonder: do people really want the Lord to alter his program so that their own earthly desires can be fulfilled? If the Lord were to pay attention to all these desires, he would never return at all!

No: in light of what the New Testament reveals, we should wake up every day with the expectation that today may be the day when we get to see him as he truly is. We should not fear that day but wait for it with joyful expectation.

I have sometimes heard respectable believers state that they have no interest in eschatology because, in the end, they know that everything will work to our benefit. I do not think that they have pondered the significance of their words. They are effectively saying that God may have an interest in revealing certain things about future events but they themselves do not. That attitude shows such a disregard for God's revelation that it pains me to hear it.

"The things to come," as the events of the future have been called, are extremely important, as these simple facts (borrowed from George Sweeting, www.preceptaustin.org/second_coming_of_christ) will show:

■ More than a quarter of the Bible is predictive prophecy.

- Approximately one third of it has yet to be fulfilled.

- Over 1,800 references to the Lord's return appear in the Old Testament, and 17 Old Testament books give prominence to this theme.

- In the 260 chapters in the New Testament, there are more than 300 references to the second coming—one in every 30 verses.

- 23 of the 27 New Testament books refer to this great event. Three of the four other books are single-chapter letters written to individuals concerning a particular subject, and the fourth is Galatians, which does imply Christ's coming again.

- For every prophecy on the first coming of Christ, there are eight on Christ's second coming.

We must study the Scriptures in order to understand the things that God has revealed about the future, but we should also know what to do while we wait for it. Jesus said, "Look, I am coming soon!" (Revelation 22:12). We'd better believe him.

A Prophetic Call to Remember

Peter has been battling false teachers who emerged from the very heart of the church. In 2 Peter 2, we saw him condemn both the conduct and the character of these teachers. In fact, 2 Peter 2 contains some of the most severe words in the Bible against those who had introduced heretical teaching into the church.

Peter now shifts his focus to contradicting the teachings which he considers very threatening to the church of his day—and which remain so for the church of today. He shows the special interest that false teachers have in denying the possibility of Christ's return. The apostle knows that if someone can be convinced that Christ will not return to judge the world of sin, it will be extremely simple to convince them to live according to the desires of the flesh. If there's one thing that characterizes an apostate, it is their immoral lifestyle, driven by desire and self-interest, which is completely contrary to the fruit of the Spirit in the believer.

In 2 Peter 3, Peter does something similar to what he did at the beginning of chapter 1. He calls the believers to remember. Over time, we tend to forget the weighty doctrines of the faith. Therefore, before Peter addresses the significance of the second coming of Christ, he insists one more time on the need to remember:

> "Dear friends, this is now my second letter to you. I have written both of them as reminders to stimulate you to wholesome thinking. I want you to recall the words spoken in the past by the holy prophets and the command given by our Lord and Savior through your apostles." (2 Peter **3:1-2**)

Once again, Peter calls his readers "dear friends." Certainly, love for our brothers and sisters in Christ is one of the distinguishing marks of a true believer. Jesus called his disciples "friends" (John 15:15); now Peter refers to his readers in the same way.

He gives them the general reason why he has written both letters: "as reminders to stimulate you to wholesome thinking." Peter wants his readers to remember the need to think in a sober manner and to have a clear understanding about the things that have already been revealed. It is of no use to learn new truths or recall previously known truths if neither will contribute to the transformation of our lives. Our thinking must remain clear, logical, consistent, and morally pure. Peter's specific concern in this portion of his letter is to present the second coming of Christ in the future as an encouragement toward holy living now.

It is of no use to learn truth if it doesn't transform our lives.

The second coming of our Lord was announced hundreds of years before even his first coming. In case anyone questions his authority to write about the things to come, Peter reminds his readers of the source of his teaching: 1) "the holy prophets" and 2) "our Lord and Savior through the apostles." By calling the prophets "holy," Peter emphasizes that those who had this role were specially chosen by God for such a task. The same can be said of the apostles (Luke 6:12-16). Paul calls the prophets and the apostles the foundation of the church (Ephesians 2:20). Peter's point here is that what follows is authoritative teaching.

The prophets are related to the Old Testament; the testimony of the Lord Jesus Christ is related to the first part of the New Testament; and the teaching of the apostles is related to the second and last part of the New Testament. By appealing to the holy prophets, Christ, and the apostles, Peter also demonstrates the unity of the Bible.

Among other things, Peter is trying to bring to mind what his readers should have heard—if they are Jewish—in the synagogues in their early years during the reading of the Scriptures. For example:

- Isaiah gives a detailed account of the day of his coming (Isaiah 2:10-22; 24:1-6).

- Jeremiah refers to it as the "time of trouble for Jacob" (30:7).

- Daniel states, "There will be a time of distress such as has not happened from the beginning of nations until then" (Daniel 12:1).

- Joel says that the day of the Lord is near (Joel 1:15).

- Amos mentions the "day of the Lord" twice in one chapter (Amos 5:18-20).

- Zephaniah mentions that the day of the Lord is near (Zephaniah 1:7).

In the New Testament, the Lord spoke about that final day in chapters 24 and 25 of Matthew:

"When the Son of Man comes in his glory, and all the angels with him, he will sit on his glorious throne. All the nations will be gathered before him, and he will separate the people one from another as a shepherd separates the sheep from the goats. He will put the sheep on his right and the goats on his left. Then the King will say to those on his right, 'Come, you who are blessed by my Father; take your inheritance, the kingdom prepared for you since the creation of the world."

(Matthew 25:31-34)

This is not a new teaching that Peter is writing; it has been there as part of the Scriptures for hundreds of years, and it also comes from the very lips of Jesus. We must take it as seriously as any other teaching we receive in God's word.

Questions for reflection

1. In your opinion, why do so many people show so little interest in eschatology even though it is part of biblical revelation?

2. Why do you think God revealed through the prophets the second coming of Christ hundreds of years before his first coming?

3. Why do you think that even believers fear the next coming of Christ?

PART TWO

Mockers Ignore God's Revelation

The messengers of God have always been mocked and ridiculed, not only when they announced the revelation of God but even when, for example, Nehemiah and his people tried to rebuild the walls around the city of Jerusalem (Nehemiah 4:1-6). It is no surprise to see false teachers going back to the same action:

> "Above all, you must understand that in the last days scoffers will come, scoffing and following their own evil desires. They will say, 'Where is this "coming" he promised? Ever since our ancestors died, everything goes on as it has since the beginning of creation.'" (2 Peter **3:3-4**)

"The *last days*," as 20th-century minister Dick Lucas explained, "is standard New Testament shorthand for the period between the first and second coming of Jesus Christ" (R.C. Lucas and Christopher Green, *The Message of 2 Peter & Jude*, Kindle loc. 2124 of 5326). The resurrection of Jesus Christ marked the start of the last days, and they have not yet been completed.

It is characteristic of these last days that false teachers rise up. Peter refers to these individuals as "scoffers." False teachers are not simply those who express some degree of skepticism about biblical truth; they are those who are willing to mock what God has revealed. Peter also describes them as those who live to please the flesh. When we think about false teachers, we have to look at how they handle money, sex, and power. As we have already seen, the false teachers Peter was dealing with were greedy, carnal in their lifestyles, and abusive when in authority. We find the same thing today.

"Where is this 'coming' he promised?" these scoffers asked (**v 4**). They used the delay in God's judgment to affirm that he would never return. Nothing had changed since the beginning of creation, so presumably it never would. Of course, this is not consistent with the biblical record: God has come in judgment before, and he will again.

When someone is willing to lie, it becomes impossible to have a reasonable debate or even a conversation with that person. Liars are interested in affirming whatever fits their purposes; therefore, the truth has no value for them. Because they cannot disprove God's truth, they resort to mocking and scoffing at it.

Peter Contradicts His Opponents

Despite the mocking of false teachers, Peter believes in the trustworthiness of the word of God. He demonstrates this by using that same word to contradict the scoffers. Peter begins his argument by pointing out how conveniently the scoffers "deliberately forget that long ago by God's word the heavens came into being and the earth was formed out of water and by water" (**v 5**). God was at work even before Adam and Eve came into being. He prepared the world for them and their descendants. However, after some time had elapsed, humanity became so corrupt that God decided to flood the world in judgment. "By these waters also the world of that time was deluged and destroyed" (**v 6**). When the false teachers said that nothing had changed since the beginning of creation, they were ignoring this story.

> God prepared the world for Adam and Eve and their descendants. But it became corrupt.

You may be thinking: what do these scoffers who denied God's revelation have to do with me? First, these verses are a warning to us not to deny the biblical narrative. Second, we should be aware that every time we sin and continue to sin, knowing that our actions are evil, we are challenging the authority of God's word. As long as we choose to remain in our sin, we are essentially mocking God's holiness. It is like saying, "I know you revealed yourself and your truth in your word, but I choose to violate it." Or perhaps it can be compared to this other sentiment: "I love you; but for now, let me love my sin for a little while longer."

After Peter reminds the false teachers of the first global judgment—the flood—he also reminds them that the next judgment will not be merely global but universal. Both the heavens and the earth will be subject to the final judgment. Without our Savior, we would certainly not want to be present when this day arrives! "By the same word," Peter warns, "the present heavens and earth are reserved for fire, being kept for the day of judgment and destruction of the ungodly" (**v 7**). At the moment, creation is being sustained by God's word (see Hebrews 1:3). But a day will come when, by that same word, all of creation—the heavens, the earth, and all their inhabitants—will be consumed by fire. Peter says that this will be a day of judgment for the destruction of the ungodly.

The world will not end due to an atomic bomb; it is not humanity that will destroy the world. It is God himself who will cause this destruction, and with much greater force.

Why Does the Lord Delay in Coming?

Peter gives us two reasons why our Lord has not yet returned. We may use them to contradict false teachers, to answer questions from unbelievers, or to strengthen our faith—or all of the above.

Reason #1: "But do not forget this one thing, dear friends: With the Lord a day is like a thousand years, and a thousand years are like a day" (2 Peter **3:8**). The Lord lives outside of time and space. Therefore, he does not measure time as we do. Christ ascended to his throne 2,000 years ago, but in God's calendar, it is as if Christ left earth today, figuratively speaking. I say this because our Lord lives in an eternal present. Remember that his name is "I AM", not "I was" or "I will be."

Dutch theologian Herman Bavinck helps us understand this:

"We are human and he is the Lord our God. Between him and us there seems to be no such kinship or communion as would enable us to name him truthfully ... However little we know of God, even the faintest notion implies that he is a being who is infinitely exalted above every creature."

(*Reformed Dogmatics*, Vol. 2, p 30)

He is the one "who is, and who was, and who is to come" (Revelation 1:4). This phrase contains the past, the present, and the future. It encapsulates the continuous present in which God lives. Therefore, God is not delaying—not according to how he measures time. This is how Peter explains it in 2 Peter **3:9**: "The Lord is not slow in keeping his promise, as some understand slowness."

Reason #2: "Instead, he is patient with you, not wanting anyone to perish, but everyone to come to repentance" (**v 9**).

The Lord could carry out his judgment right now. But he has not done so because there are people who will come to salvation today, tomorrow, next month, and beyond. Desiring that they all come to repentance, he has delayed his judgment in our favor. What detains the Lord's judgment, in other words, is not our good behavior but his infinite goodness. The Lord is waiting for more people to come to repentance. He is delaying his judgment because of his mercy.

When He Comes

The phrase "the day of the Lord" appears 17 times in the Old Testament: twice in Isaiah (13:6; 13:9), twice in Ezekiel (13:5; 30:3), five times in Joel (1:15; 2:1, 11, 31; 3:14), three times in Amos (5:18, 20), once in Obadiah (1:15), twice in Zephaniah (1: 7, 14), once in Zechariah (14:1) and once in Malachi (4:5). It also appears four times in the New Testament (Acts 2:20; 1 Thessalonians 5:2; 2 Thessalonians 2:2; and here in 2 Peter **3:10**). If we add to our list all the occurrences of the similar phrase "the day of the Lord's wrath", the idea is found about 24 times in the entire Bible—with consistency in the way it is described.

But when will the day of the Lord take place, and what will it be like? No one is certain. We only have small pieces of the puzzle.

However, in **verse 10** Peter does give us some brief information about how some of the final episodes will play out.

1. It Will Come Like a Thief

"The day of the Lord will come like a thief." How do thieves come? They arrive suddenly and by surprise, without the homeowner realizing. A thief may be getting ready to break into your house this very evening, yet at this moment you have no way of knowing it. Likewise, Christ could come this very night, and right now you wouldn't know it. Now you still have time to give your life to Christ if you do not yet know him as your Savior and Lord. It is possible he may be only hours away from his coming, but you still have time to repent and give your life to him. But once he arrives, there will not be a single additional second for another opportunity.

The Lord Jesus describes this sudden return in the same way:

"Therefore keep watch, because you do not know on what day your Lord will come. But understand this: If the owner of the house had known at what time of night the thief was coming, he would have kept watch and would not have let his house be broken into." (Matthew 24:42-43)

2. The Earth Will Be Laid Bare

No one knows the time of Jesus' arrival; but everyone will know when he arrives. "The heavens will disappear with a roar; the elements will be destroyed by fire, and the earth and everything done in it will be laid bare" (2 Peter **3:10**). The word that is translated as "be destroyed" also means "melt" or "disintegrate". When this occurs, there will be a great roar, and suddenly, everything will be burned. Everything that exists will disappear. Can you imagine how great the roar will be when the entire universe implodes—when everything collapses?

How will this happen? It will happen in the same way that the universe was created: by the word of God. God spoke, and everything came into being. God will speak again, and everything will come undone.

Jesus gave us another bit of information in Luke 21: "There will be signs in the sun, moon and stars. On the earth, nations will be in anguish and perplexity at the roaring and tossing of the sea. People will faint from terror, apprehensive of what is coming on the world, for the heavenly bodies will be shaken. At that time they will see the Son of Man coming in a cloud with power and great glory" (v 25-27).

Sin has had such a devastating effect on God's creation that at the time of judgment, everything will be affected. The earth will be laid waste, just as we read in Isaiah 24:3: "The earth will be completely laid waste and totally plundered. The LORD has spoken this word."

When God says through Isaiah that the earth will be laid waste, he means that the earth will be emptied of people, animals, and plants. In fact, the earth itself will pass away (Matthew 24:35), and there will be a new earth (as we will see in the next chapter).

Old and New

2 Peter **3:10** has been the subject of many debates and controversies. What is meant, exactly, by this description of the end of the universe as we know it?

In the King James Version (one of the earliest English translations of the Bible), the last phrase of this verse was translated as "the earth also and the works that are therein shall be burned up." However, more recent translations have preferred a different rendering: "the earth and everything done in it will be laid bare" (NIV); "the earth and the works that are done on it will be exposed" (ESV).

Those who have been influenced by the oldest translation tend to think that God will utterly destroy everything and bring a completely new heaven and earth. However, we need to place this text next to the teachings of Paul. This is what Paul teaches in his epistle to the Romans:

"For the creation was subjected to frustration, not by its own choice, but by the will of the one who subjected it, in hope that *the creation itself will be liberated from its bondage to decay* and brought into the freedom and glory of the children of God" (Romans 8:20-21, emphasis added).

This language seems to indicate that the creation will be brought back to the condition it was in when Adam and Eve lived in the Garden of Eden—or better.

How, then, do we explain the word "new" in Revelation 21:1, where John speaks of a "new heaven and a new earth"—and in 2 Peter 3:13, which we will look at in the next chapter? Perhaps the best explanation lies in the meaning of the word "new." In the original language, two different words can be translated as "new." The first one is *neos*, which usually refers to something that has been made for the first time, like a car that has never been used. But the word used to describe the new heaven and new earth is *kainos*, which refers to something that is "new in quality and superior in character" (see Randy Alcorn, *Heaven*, p 148). It can also refer to something that is renewed. Author Randy Alcorn adds, "Interestingly enough, it is the word *kainos* that Paul uses to describe the Christian, as a new (*kainos*) creation. The individual Christian has not been vaporized into non-existence and newly created; rather the old (*archaios*) has passed away, and the new (*kainos*) has come."

This is why some speak of an entirely new creation at the end of time, while others prefer to speak of the renewal of the fallen creation. The latter is my preferred understanding.

But whichever interpretation you prefer, it is certainly clear that there will be destruction, and there will be something new. The new heavens and new earth will mark…

- the end of creation's groaning.

- the end of sinning.

- the end of pain, suffering, and tears.

- the end of deceptions and loss.

- the end of death for believers.

- the beginning of the second death for the ungodly.

Christians should live their lives crying out, "Maranata!"—a word in Aramaic which literally means, "The Lord has come," but which can also be used to say, "Come quickly, Lord."

Questions for reflection

1. Have you ever faced scoffers in your life? If so, how did you react to them? How should we react to those who scoff at God?

2. Why do you think that some believers are so timid when it comes to speaking about the final judgment?

3. How can you keep watch and be ready for the Lord's coming?

6. HOW TO WAIT FOR HIS SECOND COMING

Verses 1-10 of this final chapter of 2 Peter have given us a very succinct idea of how the world will end and how the Lord will return: unexpectedly. Other passages of the Bible give us more details about what will happen before these events take place: the appearance of the man of lawlessness (2 Thessalonians 2:1-4); the falling of many from the faith (1 Timothy 4:1) and the moral deterioration of humanity, which will go from bad to worse (2 Timothy 3:1-5, 13).

The question that we must be asking ourselves is: in the meantime, how should we await Christ's second coming? Or how do we live in this time of "now but not yet"? As Peter closes his letter, he clearly lets us know how our Lord expects us to wait for him. We will examine the text bit by bit, but first let me summarize Peter's teaching in this last portion of the chapter:

1. Peter encourages us to live in a godly manner in view of the coming judgment (2 Peter **3:11-12** and **14**).

2. Peter tries to inspire hope in us by reminding us that our next life will take place on a new earth and with a new heaven (**v 13**).

3. Peter teaches us to interpret the Lord's delay in returning not as a sign of a failed promise, as the false teachers taught, but as a sign of God's patience and mercy; the Lord is trying to save as many people as possible (**v 15-16**).

4. Peter exhorts us to be on the alert: we must be careful not to be

dragged away by false teachers and suffer the consequences that come with turning away from the Lord (**v 16-17**).

5. Peter calls us to grow in the grace and the knowledge of the Lord (**v 18**).

Wait For the Lord

This is what Peter has already told us about the second coming: "But the day of the Lord will come like a thief. The heavens will disappear with a roar; the elements will be destroyed by fire, and the earth and everything done in it will be laid bare" (v 10). This idea is completed at the end of **verse 12**, where we are told about "the destruction of the heavens by fire," when "the elements will melt in the heat."

Knowing about the coming of the Lord and his future judgment is only helpful if we know what to do in the interim. So, God used Peter to reveal to us the way we should spend our lives during this time of "now but not yet." In **verse 11**, Peter poses the question: "Since everything will be destroyed in this way, what kind of people ought you to be?" Then he immediately gives us the answer: "You ought to live holy and godly lives".

What does that lifestyle look like? Is it someone who doesn't do anything pleasurable? No! A life of "don't" was the lifestyle of the Pharisees in New Testament times, and it is that of pharisaical believers today. No, the lifestyle that reflects God's character is the one described in the beatitudes (Matthew 5:3-12). Jesus says, "Blessed are…"

- *the poor in spirit.* These are simple people—those who are truly humble. Or, to put it in other terms, these people do not consider themselves as having any special privileges or any merit.

- *those who mourn.* That is, those who are grieved by sinning against God.

- *the meek.* These are individuals who do not talk much about their achievements; they prefer to let others speak well of them.

2 Peter 3 v 11-18
2 Peter 3 v 11-18

- *those who hunger and thirst for righteousness.* This group has been declared righteous by Christ at the time of salvation, but then they love to live righteously to honor their Savior.

- *the merciful.* There is a lack of a condemnatory spirit in such people. Reflecting God's character implies treating others with the same mercy with which he has treated us.

- *the pure in heart.* Obviously, no one except the Lord is perfect or sinless. But these are people without malice, with good intentions, and with the overarching desire to live in a way that reflects the gospel.

- *the peacemakers.* These are people who love to forgive and who can easily ask for forgiveness. They are people who love reconciliation.

- *those who are persecuted.* These are people willing to suffer persecution for the cause of Christ. They are people who keep silent, just as our Lord Jesus Christ did, when others pronounce curses against them.

The idea of holy living while awaiting the coming of the Lord is reinforced in 2 Peter **3:14**: "So then, dear friends, since you are looking forward to this, make every effort to be found spotless, blameless and at peace with him." The concept of being spotless and blameless is one that goes way back. In the Old Testament, any lamb that was offered for sacrifice had to have no blemish or defect. Hebrews 9:14 explains that Christ too was an "unblemished" sacrifice; he lived spotlessly and that is why he could ultimately offer himself as a sacrifice for sins. Now God expects those of us who live in the midst of this dark world to live blameless lives. Paul tells us we are to be "blameless and pure, 'children of God without fault in a warped and crooked generation'" (Philippians 2:15). He continues, "Then you will shine among them like stars in the sky."

A New Heaven and a New Earth

In 2 Peter **3:13**, Peter reminds us that our next life will take place in a new earth and under new heavens—a place in which righteousness reigns. The author of Revelation, in chapter 22, describes this new earth as a city: the new Jerusalem (see also 21:2). Through this city flows the river of the water of life, and on each side of the river is the tree of life. This sounds very similar to the description of the Garden of Eden in Genesis. The garden was irrigated by four rivers, but the new Jerusalem has its own river. Just as there was a tree of life in the Garden of Eden, there will also be a tree of life in the new Jerusalem.

It is as if God is telling us, *I am returning creation to its original state, just as it was before the fall.*

> Earthly mansions are like straw huts compared to the places we will have on the new earth.

God's love for us in Christ is so great that even after the fall, he has redeemed us. But he is also planning to redeem the entire creation. We will live eternally with him on a new earth and under new heavens. There will be no more crying or pain, no death, and no sin. In the coming world, we will not be able to use what we have accumulated in this present world. Our current money has no value there, and our checks have no backing funds. Our earthly mansions, no matter how big they may be, are like straw huts compared to the places we will have on the new earth.

And this new creation is "where righteousness dwells" (2 Peter **3:13**). This is the kingdom of God which Jesus spoke about. This means that the day of the Lord will be not only a fearful day of judgment but a great day of celebration. We will rejoice...

- as we see Jesus in all his glory.

- at the consummation of history.

- at the fulfillment of every prophecy related to the final day.

■ at the liberation of the entire creation from its bondage and decay (Romans 8:20-21)!

Peter is highlighting two closely related motivations for a life of holiness and godliness. First, we are to avoid sin because, as we look forward to the second coming, we take seriously the threat of judgment. This day of accountability is for everyone—which calls for sobriety. Second, we are to live lives that are righteous in order to reflect the new order that will be inaugurated with the coming of the Lord.

You may be surprised that Peter uses the day of judgment and the coming of the Lord as motivation for us to live holy lives. John Calvin, the great Reformer, explains the need for this motivation: it shakes us awake.

> "*But the day of the Lord will come.* This has been added, that the faithful might be always watching ... so [Peter] now shakes off our sleepiness, so that we may attentively expect Christ at all times, lest we should become idle and negligent, as it is usually the case. For whence is it that flesh indulges itself except that there is no thought of the near coming of Christ?"
>
> (*Commentaries on the Catholic Epistles*, 8.4.3)

Calvin is making the point that when we do not keep fresh in our minds the coming of the Lord and the judgment that he will bring, our flesh surrenders to its own desires.

Paul helps us understand how this works when he writes to Titus:

> "For the grace of God has appeared that offers salvation to all people. It teaches us to say 'No' to ungodliness and worldly passions, and to live self-controlled, upright and godly lives in this present age, while we wait for the blessed hope—the appearing of the glory of our great God and Savior, Jesus Christ."
>
> (Titus 2:11-13)

The grace of God has saved us, and it is his grace that enables us to say no to worldly desires. Paul's exhortation to Titus and to all of us is to live "self-controlled, upright and godly lives ... while we wait for ... the appearing of [his] glory." We have to deny ourselves the enjoyment of sinful pleasures; we are only able to do this by the training that comes from his grace, but it is nevertheless our responsibility.

Hence, Paul instructed Timothy, "Train yourself to be godly" (1 Timothy 4:7). Notice how Paul does not assume that the salvation received by Timothy will automatically produce a godly and holy character. No! Timothy needs training. That must mean gradual growth. This is how sanctification occurs: gradually, via training, with the goal of developing a disciplined life. Paul and Peter both teach us that one of the ways to train ourselves to live a self-controlled, upright and godly life is to reflect on the glorious manifestation of our Lord that is to come.

Given the magnitude of the events, given the temporariness of everything that exists, and given the certainty of the final day, God expects our way of life to be exceptionally holy. The expectation of his return and his judgment should produce in us a lifestyle that is consistent not with this world but with the world that is coming—where holiness will reign.

This means…

- we should be a people who acknowledge that we have no merit before a holy God.

- we should be a people who realize that we are unworthy of occupying any position in the kingdom of heaven.

A godly life is one that is characterized by the mourning of our own sin. We can no longer live as though our sins are insignificant. Adopting the lifestyle of the inhabitants of this world while knowing that it will be destroyed makes no sense. It is inconsistent with the future that awaits us. What's more, adopting the lifestyle of this age would be inviting God's judgment on us. Instead, as God's children we should be exhibiting a lifestyle that reflects his character and strives to be worthy of his approval. In this way we will "shine … like stars in the sky."

Questions for reflection

1. Do you feel excited or afraid about the second coming of the Lord? What are some reasons why you feel one way or another?

2. What are your thoughts on the statement made by Calvin, on page 89, about our need to be reminded about the second coming of Christ as a motivator for holy living?

3. In your life this week, what will it look like to live mindful of that final day?

PART TWO

Motivators for Holy Living

Before we move on, it is worth reviewing some other teachings used by God to motivate a life of obedience in us. We certainly need multiple reminders and motivations in order to live a life of holiness and godliness, and the Bible bears witness to this truth. Here in 2 Peter, the encouragement for living in holiness is Christ's second coming and the judgment that will bring the destruction of the world. As we review the biblical narrative, we can see that God uses several other ideas to motivate us to walk in holiness.

The holiness of God is the motivation for holy living in Leviticus 11:44 and 20:7, and in 1 Peter 1:15-16, which highlights God's command to "be holy, because I am holy." The implication is that God does not negotiate on the holiness of his own being. This means he doesn't simply overlook our sin in order somehow to show us that he really loves us. Rather, because he truly loves us, he cannot turn a blind eye to our sin. He knows that it would eventually destroy us. So he calls us to be holy.

In Leviticus 19, the expression "I am the Lord your God" appears 16 times as a way of emphasizing God's holy name. The late Jerry Bridges comments, "That repetition of his holy name in Leviticus 19 appears as a reminder that obedience to his statutes and laws must flow as a result of reverence and fear of the Lord" (*The Practice of Godliness*, p 13). The holy and righteous character of the God whom we represent is the motivation for holiness.

And yet this does not represent the entire counsel of God. He calls us to be holy in other ways, too:

- In Philippians 1:27, the motivation for holiness is the gospel: our call is to live in a way worthy of the gospel.

- In John 14:15, the motivation for obedience and sanctification is our love for Christ: "If you love me, keep my commandments."

▪ In Hebrews 12:26-29, the motivation for the life of godliness is again the coming of Christ and the final judgment.

Take note of the following words from the author of Hebrews:

"At that time his voice shook the earth, but now he has promised, 'Once more I will shake not only the earth but also the heavens.' The words 'once more' indicate the removing of what can be shaken—that is, created things—so that what cannot be shaken may remain. Therefore, since we are receiving a kingdom that cannot be shaken, let us be thankful, and so worship God acceptably with reverence and awe, for our 'God is a consuming fire.'" (Hebrews 12:26-29)

The same author who reminds us that we must approach the throne of grace with confidence (Hebrews 4:16) is also the one who reminds us that our God, whom we approach with confidence, is a consuming fire. He is encouraging us to offer worship to God as an acceptable sacrifice; this speaks of our living out lives of godliness. But the motivation for the life of godliness is the coming of the one who is defined as a consuming fire and "the removing of what can be shaken."

> We should have a sense of joy—but a sense of fear at the same time.

There should certainly be a sense of joy in believers as we think of our coming Lord, but there should also be a sense of fear at the same time. What do I mean by that? John Murray, the founder of Westminster Theological Seminary, tells us:

"What or whom we worship determines our behavior. What then is the fear of God? There are at least two distinct senses in which the word 'fear' is used in Scripture … 1) The fear of being afraid of God and his punitive judgments; 2) the fear of reverential awe and adoration" (*Principles of Conduct*, p 231).

As children of God, we fear God in the second sense. The punishment for our sin has been taken in its entirety by Jesus on the cross, and we have nothing to fear from God. But we must understand that all disobedience constitutes an affront against the dignity of the God who is capable of destroying all his creation for having been corrupted by sin. In that sense we fear God—and we seek to live lives worthy of him.

God's Patience Delays His Coming

In 2 Peter **3:15-16**, Peter speaks to us once again about seeing the Lord's delay in returning not as a sign that he will fail to fulfill his promise but as a sign of his patience in seeking the salvation of many: "Bear in mind that our Lord's patience means salvation, just as our dear brother Paul also wrote you with the wisdom that God gave him."

God is more concerned with the fate of the unsaved than we are. According to Peter, the reason Christ has not returned yet is because he will save many more before he does. This also explains why Jesus gave us the Great Commission to take the gospel to the ends of the earth. And that's why we are told in Romans 10:14-15, "How, then, can they call on the one they have not believed in? And how can they believe in the one of whom they have not heard? And how can they hear without someone preaching to them? And how can anyone preach unless they are sent? As it is written: 'How beautiful are the feet of those who bring good news!'"

Paul had spoken in his letters about the fact that the Lord's patience must be counted as his desire to save sinners: "Or do you show contempt for the riches of his kindness, forbearance and patience, not realizing that God's kindness is intended to lead you to repentance?" (Romans 2:4). He had also taught, "Where sin increased, grace increased all the more" (5:20). As we might expect, his opponents had distorted these teachings (2 Peter **3:16**). It seems that they were teaching "cheap grace"—saying that it doesn't matter how much someone sins, since God will always forgive them. Paul himself responded to this teaching with a strong declaration: "Shall we go on sinning so that grace may increase? By no means! We are those who have died to sin; how can we live in it any longer?" (Romans 6:1-2).

Peter calls out the false teachers who misuse and distort Paul's teaching: they are "ignorant and unstable." They also distort the message of the rest of the Scriptures about the Lord's coming and the reason why he has not yet come. In the Old Testament, we are shown in multiple passages that God is slow to anger: Exodus 34:6; Numbers 14:18; Psalm 86:15; Jonah 4:2, among others. There will be a final judgment, but the goodness of God has put the brakes on that judgment for the moment because God does not take pleasure in the death of the wicked (Ezekiel 33:11), and much less in the punishment of his children. It is the goodness of God that leads us to repentance. It is his patience that allows many to be saved.

Be on the Alert

Next, Peter exhorts us to be vigilant. We must not be seduced by the proclaimed lies of false teachers and suffer the consequences of turning away from the Lord.

> "Therefore, dear friends, since you have been forewarned, be on
> your guard so that you may not be carried away by the error of
> the lawless and fall from your secure position." (2 Peter **3:17**)

Once again, Peter calls his followers "dear friends". He is concerned about them. Every pastor who has a shepherd's heart and knows the Scriptures worries about the possibility of his sheep being carried away by deceivers. This concern was even more evident in Peter's heart as he drew nearer to his departure from this world into glory.

Peter probably remembered how, at one point, he was confronted by Paul for his hypocrisy in being unwilling to associate with Gentiles out of fear of the Jews. Peter had received a vision from God telling him that he should not consider the Gentiles as unclean and that he should be willing to associate with them. He was highly criticized for embracing them, and yet he defended the lesson of the vision (Acts 10 – 11). Yet, some time later, he apparently forgot the implications of the vision he had received. The situation became worse, as Paul explains in Galatians 2:13: "The other Jews joined him in his hypocrisy, so that by their hypocrisy even **Barnabas** was led astray." This proves just how easy it is for Christians—even Christian leaders—to go wrong. Paul confronted Peter when he saw that he was "not acting in line with the truth of the gospel" (Galatians 2:14). So Peter knew firsthand the value of being corrected when you have gone wrong.

It is hard to imagine a pastor with a true shepherd's heart who would not be concerned enough about his sheep to warn them about false teachers and their influence. Peter is concerned. He says that he is worried that some of his readers will fall from their "secure position" (2 Peter **3:17**). In other words, the fact that we stand firm today does not guarantee that we will stand firm tomorrow. The steadfastness of the believer comes from clinging to the word of God. When we stray from the word, we are wandering either into doctrinal errors or into sinful practices. The shepherd who loves his sheep cares about both.

Continue to Grow until He Returns

Finally, Peter calls us to grow in the grace and knowledge of the Lord. Growing in grace means growing into the image of the Lord. Many Christians have been in the faith for years but have grown little in grace. In other words, despite many years in the Christian faith, their resemblance to the character of the Lord Jesus Christ has not improved much.

If we want to know what a Christian who has grown in grace looks like, we need only read Galatians 5:22-23: "But the fruit of the Spirit is love, joy, peace, forbearance, kindness, goodness, faithfulness, gentleness and self-control. Against such things there is no law."

Ask yourself the following questions:

■ Am I growing in my ability to love others?

■ How much joy do I experience in my daily life?

■ Is inner peace something that I experience?

2 Peter 3 v 11-18

- How much have I grown in patience toward others and, especially, toward those who have sinned against me?

- How gentle or kind have I been today in dealing with others?

- Have I grown in humility or meekness?

- How often do I look at others and think that they are proud?

- How am I doing with self-control?

- Am I in control of my sinful impulses?

- How well am I controlling my anger?

- How do I speak to others?

These questions may help you know if you are growing in grace. As you reflect on them, ask God to help you to grow in any area in which you feel you are deficient.

Finally, Peter tells us that we must grow in the knowledge of the Lord. This is not simply growing in biblical knowledge but in knowledge of God's character. This is what transforms us because as we get to know God, we become more like him. The Spirit of God helps us grow in the likeness of our Lord.

Don't forget that our call is to live a holy and godly life, and that requires us as believers to be devoted to God. As we come to the end of 2 Peter and reflect on the way we should live while waiting for the appearing of our Lord of lords, a good way to close is to quote the 18th-century writer William Law, who defines devotion this way:

"Devotion signifies a life given, or devoted, to God. The devout, therefore, are those who live no longer [according] to their own will, or the way and spirit of the world, but live [according] to the sole will of God, consider God in everything and serve God in everything. They are devout who make all the parts of their common life parts of piety, by doing everything in the name of God, and under such rules as are conformable to his Glory."

(*A Serious Call to a Devout and Holy Life*, p 5)

"To him be glory both now and forever!" Peter tells us (2 Peter **3:18**). We may echo, "Amen."

Questions for reflection

1. Are you on the alert regarding false teachings and your own spiritual growth? If so, how? If not, how could you be more alert?

2. Reflect on your spiritual growth over the past year or two. How have you changed? What would you most like to grow in over the next year or two?

3. How can you grow in devotion to God this week?

7. CONTEND FOR THE FAITH

The epistles of 2 Peter and Jude have much in common. Much discussion has taken place about who borrowed material from whom—or whether there may even have been a third source that both authors used. Wherever the material originated, however, it is clear that in both cases, the authors were writing against false teachers, who were threatening the doctrine of the church and seeking to influence believers to live sinfully.

- Both letters speak of morally and doctrinally corrupt teachers.

- Both contain warnings about the judgment of God, using the example of fallen angels whom God has kept in dark prisons.

- Both therefore warn that God will not ignore the harm caused by these false teachers; they should certainly expect punishment.

- Both authors mention that these false teachers reject authority and dare to mock heavenly or angelic beings.

- Both refer to these false teachers as people who talk about what they do not understand and who do so instinctively, as if they were irrational animals.

- Both letters mention that these false teachers live in sin even while they feast and eat with true believers.

- Peter refers to false teachers as springs without water, while Jude refers to them as clouds without water.

■ Both Peter and Jude say that in the last days mockers with sinful desires will arise.

Jude is estimated to have been written in the year AD 65. It is a short, intense, and defiant wake-up call with a great sense of urgency. Despite its brevity, it has some interesting features: notably its use of triplets of words or phrases. The following list is adapted from G.P. Waugh's commentary on 2 Peter:

■ The recipients of the letter are described as called, loved, and kept (Jude **v 1**).

■ The greeting contains a triple blessing: "Mercy, peace, and love" (**v 2**).

■ There are three examples of judgments: Israel in the wilderness, angels in prisons of darkness, and the punishment of Sodom and Gomorrah (**v 5-7**).

■ Jude outlines three characteristics of apostates: they "pollute their own bodies, reject authority and heap abuse on celestial beings" (v 8).

■ He refers to three people who paid for their sins: Cain, Balaam, and Korah (v 11).

■ There are six metaphors to describe false teachers: they are blemishes at love feasts, shepherds who feed only themselves, clouds without rain, autumn trees without fruit and uprooted, wild waves of the sea foaming up their shame, and wandering stars (v 12-13).

■ The three Persons of the Trinity are mentioned: the Holy Spirit, God, and Christ (v 20-21).

■ Jude recommends three spiritual exercises: building yourselves up, praying, and keeping yourself in God's love (v 20-21).

■ There are three kinds of sheep to consider: those in doubt, those in danger of fire, and those that are corrupted (v 22-23).

Who Was Jude?

Like Peter, Jude identifies himself at the beginning of the letter—as was typical in ancient times. He identifies himself first as a servant of Jesus Christ and second as James' brother.

There was a James among the twelve apostles, but most believe that Jude is identifying himself not with this James (who was the brother of John and the son of Zebedee) but with James the half brother of Jesus, who was never one of the Twelve, but who later became the head of the church in Jerusalem. This would mean that Jude, too, was a half brother of Jesus. Sure enough, in Matthew 13:55 and Mark 6:3 we read that Jesus had four brothers, whose names were James, Joseph, Simon, and Jude. John 7:5 and Mark 3:21 tells us that these brothers did not believe in Jesus and even said that he was out of his mind. But it seems they came to faith soon after the death and resurrection of Jesus—they are included among the believers in Acts 1:14.

It is significant then that Jude does not identify himself as a brother of Jesus but rather as his servant, emphasizing the spiritual relationship he has with Christ rather than the biological one. It is more important to be a brother of Jesus spiritually than biologically! Jesus himself said, "Whoever does the will of my Father in heaven is my brother and sister and mother" (Matthew 12:50).

Moreover, when Jude says that he is a servant of Jesus Christ, he is placing himself in a position of subordination, as Douglas Moo explains:

> "'Servant' can also be translated 'slave'—the Greek word is not *diakonos* ('[household] servant') but *doulos* ('[bond] slave'). The word obviously indicates Jude's subservience to the Lord whom he has come to know and to whom he now gives himself in service." (*Jude*, Kindle loc. 5177 of 7745)

Jude was a person of pre-eminent position and renown, yet this was not how he introduced himself.

Beginning with Blessings

Immediately after his introduction, Jude shows his heart for his readers by pronouncing three distinct blessings from God: "Mercy, peace, and love be yours in abundance" (Jude **v 2**). Wishing them mercy is another way of wishing that God's goodness be with them in the midst of a society which was antagonistic to the Christian faith. His wish for them is that God would protect them while they endured adversity—and that they would have peace. Jude was aware that the peace Christ promised them did not depend on the circumstances surrounding the believers; it was not something the world could produce. No, this peace is an emotional stability produced by the indwelling Holy Spirit as the result of us believing that our God is in control of all events. This is why Jesus said, "Peace I leave with you; my peace I give you. I do not give to you as the world gives" (John 14:27).

The brothers and sisters Jude was addressing were suffering persecution. They were going to have to love each other and love their enemies. Since love comes from God, it would be vital for them to experience the love of the Father in an increasing way in order to love and protect each other, and even to love those who were persecuting them.

But we can say without a doubt that this letter was also written for a universal audience: Christians throughout the centuries. Look again at Jude **v 1**: Jude addresses a group characterized as "those who have been called, who are loved in God the Father and kept for Jesus Christ." We are part of that group, along with the rest of our brothers and sisters in Christ.

These three words—"called," "loved," and "kept"—speak about how great our privileges are in Christ.

We were called from before the foundation of the world, according to Romans 8:28 and in Ephesians 1:4. God chose us in Jesus Christ before creating the universe. He conceived us in his mind and from eternity past called us to salvation and consequently to be conformed to the image of his Son. The certainty of our final destiny is therefore not guaranteed by our degree of obedience, although we do owe total obedience to our Lord. The guarantee comes from God himself, who called us before we had even drawn our first breaths.

Those who have been called are also those "who are loved in God the Father." God did not love us because of any special condition within us; he just decided to do so. True love does not love others because of what they do. God loves simply because it is in his nature to love; that is what true love is. This is why Christ told us that if we love only those who love us, we have no merits (Matthew 5:46).

Finally, we are told that the letter is being sent to those who are being "kept for Jesus Christ." God the Father loves us, but he loves his Son as well. So, he is preserving a redeemed people who will honor and glorify his Son for the rest of eternity.

The Purpose of the Letter

Not every book or letter of the Bible clearly spells out the purpose for which it was written. But this one does. We can see Jude's motivation in one single verse:

> "Dear friends, although I was very eager to write to you about
> the salvation we share, I felt compelled to write and urge you
> to contend for the faith that was once for all entrusted to
> God's holy people." (Jude **v 3**)

Originally, Jude wanted to encourage his readers regarding the salvation that we all have in common as a result of the unconditional love of the Father for those he has chosen and saved in Christ. Perhaps he wanted to write about how privileged those who have been chosen for salvation are. However, he felt "compelled" to change his initial intention for the letter and instead to speak about the need to defend the faith. The word translated "compelled" comes from the Greek word *ananke*, which literally means "necessity." Jude *needs* to write about the defense of the faith.

This faith was "once for all entrusted to God's holy people." With this vital phrase, Jude makes us aware that there is no place for new doctrinal teaching. We have already received the completed revelation that we need for our salvation and subsequent sanctification. The New Testament often conveys this idea, emphasizing that we must maintain the purity of the faith. This is why Paul wrote to the Corinthians, "For what I received I passed on to you as of first importance" (1 Corinthians 15:3)—suggesting that he had not altered the gospel in any possible way.

It is worth noticing the word translated from Greek as "contend." It is *epagonizomai*. We get our word "agonize" from the same root as this word, which literally means "to struggle" or "to fight." This shows how intense Jude's call is to defend the faith against the theological and moral corruption that false teachers have brought into the church. False teachers have always plagued God's people with apparently new revelations or new insights about God's revelation. But since we already have a faith that has been entrusted to us "once for all," we must struggle to defend it against false additions and reinterpretations. Later, beginning in Jude v 17, Jude will speak about how we do this.

In his commentary on Jude, David Helm says the following about Jude's battle cry:

> "On your feet. The time for leisure is past. Contend. Agonize.
> Exert maximum effort. The Christian faith, in all its fullness and
> completeness, is worthy of your struggle."
>
> *(1 & 2 Peter and Jude*, p 297)

The Corruption of False Teachers

When he talks about contending for the faith, Jude is not just referring to the act of believing in Christ but to that of embracing the whole will of God (Acts 20:27). This is why Christians not only contend to defend the doctrine of the Trinity, the divinity of Christ, the crucifixion and resurrection, the second coming, and so on; we also contend for every passage that calls us to obedience. We need to defend not only the doctrines of the Christian faith but their implications. For example,

Christ's cross demands that we live a cross-shaped life. If anyone denies any of the tenets of the Christian faith or tries to weaken a passage which calls us to obey, we as God's children are under an obligation to reject that teaching.

This is the kind of false teaching which Jude himself was rejecting. His opponents were antinomians (*anti* meaning "against" and *nomos* meaning "law"): that is, they were against God's commands. He says that they "pervert the grace of our God into a license for immorality." In other words, they claimed that believers could live as they wish, counting on God's grace to forgive them in the future. But God did not give us his grace to encourage us to sin freely and without fear; he gave it to empower us to obey all of his commandments.

In Jude **v 4**, Jude's concern is plain as he describes the moral and doctrinal corruption of the false teachers.

These were wicked, incredulous, unrighteous individuals: "ungodly people" who were abusing God's grace in order to live unbridled lives. A single word, *aselgeia*, is translated by the phrase "a license for immorality." It refers to unashamed excess and the absence of moderation—completely letting oneself go—especially in sexual matters. This was what the false teachers did, claiming that God would forgive them by grace. Not only this, but they caused others to sin as well. They had "secretly slipped in" to the church, misleading the believers. They could be compared to termites which infiltrate the foundations of a building, where no one can see them, and start to ascend up the walls and through pipes, suddenly appearing in the upper floors and bringing with them destruction of any furniture, wood, or books along their path.

> They are like termites: suddenly appearing and bringing destruction.

These men had also denied the authority of the Lord Jesus Christ. Their doctrine, as well as their behavior, was wrong.

Doctrinal corruption and moral corruption often go together. Doctrine gives us the framework in which we construct our lifestyles, so bad doctrine will lead to sinful living. Or it can work the other way around: when someone starts to become morally corrupt, sooner or later they will start distorting the word of God in order to justify their immoral actions.

When our Lord Jesus made us free, he did it so that we would stop being slaves to sin. But those who distort the truth have abused God's grace and have considered this freedom given to us as a license to sin and not be subject to God's law and authority. The lifestyles of these and all false disciples deny Jesus as Sovereign Lord. It is possible to speak well of Jesus and live in a way that is completely contradictory to what Jesus taught. In fact, Titus 1:16 speaks of people who "claim to know God, but by their actions they deny him."

These were "ungodly people," those "whose condemnation was written about long ago" (Jude **v 4**). Their punishment was yet to reach them, but their destiny was certain.

Questions for reflection

1. How has the concept of being called, loved, and kept helped you in your walk with the Lord?

2. Christology, or the understanding of who Jesus is, has been attacked many times throughout church history. Why do you think this doctrine in particular comes under fire so often?

3. Do you think Christians today are ready to really contend for their faith? What might this look like for you?

PART TWO

"I don't know how you can believe in a God who wants to
condemn most of the planet … to a fiery hell."

Those words were posted on social media by Aaron Rodgers, the NFL
quarterback for the Green Bay Packers, a few years ago. Rodgers had
been raised as a Christian, but he was now asserting that he could not
believe in a God who would condemn anyone.

But if there is one thing that the Bible points out from the beginning, it is that while God is slow to anger, he is not *without* anger. This
is the way in which God revealed himself to Moses at their encounter
on Mount Sinai. He described himself as "the compassionate and gra-
cious God, slow to anger, abounding in love and faithfulness, maintaining love to thousands, and forgiving wickedness, rebellion and
sin." Then he added, "Yet he does not leave the guilty unpunished"
(Exodus 34:6-7).

I cannot imagine anyone who, in their right mind, might believe
in or applaud a government which saw rampantly increasing evil and
did not care to apply the law in order to bring about justice, preserve
order, and look after its citizens. Likewise, I cannot picture myself believing in a God who continually sees homicide, the rape of boys and
girls, public and private administrative corruption, injustice against the
weak, robbery, and countless other crimes—only to turn a blind eye
and send the perpetrators to an eternity of joy. No, there must be a
place to send the wicked: those who have not had their sins forgiven
by believing in Christ's sacrifice.

In Jude **v 5-10** Jude uses three stories from the Old Testament to
remind his readers of this very thing: there is no way for false teachers
to escape God's judgment. Their wickedness has reached such intoler-
able levels that the abundantly merciful God will finally allow his wrath
to fall upon them.

Jude starts by saying that he is going to speak to his readers about
some truths that they already know but which he finds necessary to

review (**v 5**). Once again, we are presented with the importance of remembering what has been learned, as we saw in 2 Peter 1:12.

First Example: Wilderness Rebellion

The first example comes in Jude **v 5**: "The Lord at one time delivered his people out of Egypt, but later destroyed those who did not believe." This verse speaks about how the Lord, in his mercy, took the Israelite people out of Egypt. But it also tells us that this same loving God destroyed those who did not believe while they were in the desert. In one verse we can see both God's wrath and God's mercy.

The reason for their destruction was their unbelief. The Lord parted the Red Sea so that the people could cross to the other side and avoid death at the hands of the Egyptians. He also provided manna so that they would be fed. During the day, he shielded them from the desert sun with a cloud, and at night he provided a pillar of fire to give them light. Yet none of this succeeded in growing their faith. They died and were buried in the desert because of their unbelief. This is also the case with false teachers; their unbelief will lead them to their destruction.

Unbelief is not simply ignorance or lack of understanding. It is rebellion against God; it is believing that we have a better understanding than the Creator. So it leads us to follow false teachers and not God.

Jude may have been alluding to the worship of the golden calf in place of God (Exodus 32). Alternatively, he could have been thinking of the disbelief of ten of the twelve spies who were sent to inspect the promised land (Numbers 13 – 14). These men challenged God by not believing his promise to give them the land as an inheritance. The giants occupying the land intimidated them; the spies saw them as "larger" than God. The giants in the land were the tool used to test their faith. Likewise, the things that we perceive as giants, and unconquerable in our lives, test our faith and commitment to God. And if we do not believe God, whom will we believe? There is only one possibility: false teachers.

Here is what God said to these spies and those who followed them in their rebellion:

"But as for you, your bodies will fall in this wilderness. Your children will be shepherds here for forty years, suffering for your unfaithfulness, until the last of your bodies lies in the wilderness. For forty years—one year for each of the forty days you explored the land—you will suffer for your sins and know what it is like to have me against you.' I, the LORD, have spoken, and I will surely do these things to this whole wicked community, which has banded together against me. They will meet their end in this wilderness; here they will die." (Numbers 14:32-35)

These are hard words from God: but not harder than the people's hearts.

God does not want us to forget what happened in the desert some 3,500 years ago. In the New Testament we find several other references to it. In Hebrews 3:16-19, the author writes, "Who were they who heard and rebelled? Were they not all those Moses led out of Egypt? And with whom was he angry for forty years? Was it not with those who sinned, whose bodies perished in the wilderness? And to whom did God swear that they would never enter his rest if not to those who disobeyed? So we see that they were not able to enter, because of their unbelief." Clearly, what led to the judgment upon the people was their unbelief in spite of all they had seen.

In 1 Corinthians 10:6-11, when Paul refers to this act of judgment, he calls upon the believers to…

- not be idolaters.

- not be sexually immoral.

- not put the Lord to the test.

- not grumble or complain.

Paul's implication is that the thing that brought about the people's idolatry, sexual immorality, and spirit of complaining was unbelief in

God's promises. God showed them his power, his love, his grace, his mercy, and his desire to bring them to a land of rest, all to no avail.

Yet before we judge that generation too severely, we should acknowledge that we, too, often do not believe—which in many ways is even worse, since we have received more revelation than they did. Our unbelief often manifests itself through idolatry, sexual immorality, grumbling, and ungratefulness. We affirm that God is in control, but then we seek to control our lives and the lives of others ourselves.

> We affirm that God is in control, then seek to control our lives ourselves.

Paul reminds us that the judgment upon the wilderness generation "occurred as examples to keep us from setting our hearts on evil things as they did" (1 Corinthians 10:6). God left in print the fate they suffered in order to teach us that we should not desire things considered evil by God. These stories from the Old Testament serve to instruct, admonish, and warn all at the same time.

Second Example: Fallen Angels

The second example of judgment is mentioned in Jude **v 6**: "And the angels who did not keep their positions of authority but abandoned their proper dwelling—these he has kept in darkness, bound with everlasting chains for judgment on the great Day."

We have already seen a reference to these angels in 2 Peter 2:4. They sinned in the days of Noah, probably by having children with human women (see Genesis 6:2, and my earlier discussion on page 49), and were therefore imprisoned by God. In Jude's time, this interpretation of Genesis 6:2 as referring to angelic beings was well known. So, as commentator Peter Davids points out, "The strangeness of the tradition to our ears does not mean that it was strange to Jude's readers" (*The Letters of 2 Peter and Jude*, p 49).

God gave these angelic beings a position of authority under him, but they "abandoned their proper dwelling"—in other words, they did not submit to God's authority and keep the place he had given them. They wanted more. This is why Jude uses them as an example to unmask the false teachers. These teachers, too, did not submit themselves to the authority of our Lord Jesus Christ—as we saw in Jude **v 4**.

Brothers and sisters, when we sin knowingly—and moreover, when we continue the practice of sin—this represents rebellion against our Lord's authority. Likewise, the moment we doubt God's revelation, we are beginning to stop submitting to Christ's authority, and this will lead us in a direction that will make us stumble and fall.

General Booth, the founder of the Salvation Army, warned us of this more than a hundred years ago:

> "The chief danger that confronts the coming century will be religion without the Holy Ghost, Christianity without Christ, forgiveness without repentance, salvation without regeneration, politics without God, heaven without hell."
>
> (Quoted on back cover of Iain Murray, *The Old Evangelicalism*)

We must beware of wanting a custom-made God.

Third Example: Sodom and Gomorrah

Verse 7 contains the third example of judgment: that of Sodom and Gomorrah. God's judgment on these cities is described in Genesis 18 and 19. They were characterized by sexual immorality; their inhabitants corrupted themselves and pursued "sexual immorality and perversion" (Jude **v 7**).

Some believe that this phrase alludes directly to the practice of homosexuality: God did not create human sexuality to be practiced between those of the same sex, so homosexuality is a perversion (or distortion) of his design. Others believe that this phrase is referring to the desire of certain men in Sodom to have sexual relations with the angels who visited Abraham in human form. Angels really are in a different category from humans, and this could be the reason for the use of the phrase "sexual immorality and perversion."

This interpretation would suggest a clear link between **verses 6** and **7**. First Jude refers to fallen angels who wanted to have sexual relations with human women, and second he speaks of humans desiring to have relations with angels, which is the same sin, but in reverse.

God considered the sin of the people of Sodom and Gomorrah to be so perverse that he destroyed both cities by fire. Toward the southern end of the Dead Sea, there are some hills where archeological evidence has been found of cities that were suddenly destroyed by fire around the time that the Bible records the destruction of Sodom and Gomorrah taking place. Some believe that this could be the remains of Sodom and Gomorrah themselves.

The three examples stated by Jude as illustrations of judgment or God's wrath deal with...

- unbelief—in the case of the Jewish people in the desert.

- rebellion or lack of submission to Christ's authority—in the case of the angels who are in prisons of darkness.

- sexual immorality—in the case of Sodom and Gomorrah.

Jude tells us, "They serve as an example" (**v 7**). All three sins have met with judgment in the past. We can be sure that those who practice the same sins today will meet with judgment, too.

The Wrath of Our Merciful God

It may seem paradoxical to think that a God who is infinitely merciful also has the capacity to become angrier than any other being in the universe.

The best illustration I have heard about how God can experience emotions that are seemingly opposite at the same time was from John Piper in a conference where he was teaching on the pleasures of God. He invited us to think about what happens during a hurricane. On the surface, the ocean looks utterly furious, with enormous waves. Yet just a few yards below the surface, it is completely calm. In 2004, Hurricane Ivan caused great hardships in the Caribbean islands, where it reached Category 5 status, as well as in the United States where it made landfall as a Category 3 storm. While it travelled across the Caribbean, 100-foot waves were registered—and that is not even the record! It is difficult to think that the ocean could be completely calm just a few yards beneath 100-foot waves. Yet it was.

This gives us an idea of how our God can simultaneously possess unconditional love for those who believe his promises and be extremely angry with those who corrupt his design and violate his law. To violate God's law is to dishonor his character—something God does not take lightly. Such was the lifestyle of the false teachers Jude was battling.

Questions for reflection

1. Why do you think people today find it so difficult to believe in God's judgment?

2. Which of Peter's three examples in verses 5-7 pose the greatest challenge to you personally, and to your church, today?

3. What do you think is the role of the Christian community in helping you to stay on course?

8. WOE TO FALSE TEACHERS

Jude has reminded us of three examples of God's judgment from the Old Testament. He now seeks to show us that the false teachers of his own time are every bit as deserving of punishment. He begins in **verse 8** with another set of three: the three activities carried out by the false teachers who have infiltrated the church.

These false teachers are basing their behavior on dreams instead of on the revealed word of God (**v 8**). The same thing happened during Old Testament times (see Jeremiah 23:25-26), and it still happens today. Many teachers and pastors do not teach from the pulpit what the word of God reveals; instead, they recount dreams and their own interpretations of them. Based on their dreams, these false teachers "pollute their own bodies, reject authority and heap abuse on celestial beings."

Some commentators believe that these false teachers were cursing God's angels. Others think that the "celestial beings" were more likely to be fallen angels. These false teachers presumed to have great power and authority, which, they thought, enabled them to speak against these angelic beings. This is similar to what we see today when some false teachers mock demons and brag while casting out demons from a person (see my discussion on page 57).

Compare that arrogant attitude with what Jude tells us in **verse 9**: "But even the archangel Michael, when he was disputing with the devil about the body of Moses, did not himself dare to condemn him for slander but said, 'The Lord rebuke you!'"

Michael is mentioned in the Bible in several other places:

- Daniel 10:13, as "one of the chief princes".

- Daniel 10:21, as "your prince" (that is, Israel's prince).

- Daniel 12:1, as "the great prince" who protects Israel.

- Revelation 12:7, where it is stated that Michael and his angels battled against the dragon and his angels, which represent Satan and his demons.

All of this leads us to understand that there is a real spiritual battle being waged, involving powerful angelic beings and occurring in the heavenly places.

False teachers refuse God's authority and "heap abuse on celestial beings." But the archangel Michael represents the opposite end of the spectrum: that is, submission to God's authority. For that reason, he did not dare to pronounce judgment against the devil when he was disputing about the body of Moses.

No other reference to this event is made in the Bible. However, in Jewish literature, there is a book called *The Assumption of Moses*, which the early church knew and believed. (We'll discuss Jude's use of non-biblical literature further later in this chapter.) In this book's narration, the archangel Michael is the one who buried Moses. Satan tries to steal the body of Moses from Michael, and while he is doing this, instead of cursing or mocking Satan, the only thing Michael dares to say is, "May the Lord rebuke you." This shows respect for and submission to God's authority. The archangel Michael maintained his place of submission when the time came to contend with Satan. He left the judgment to God.

Jude wanted to demonstrate that if even Michael, an archangel, was careful when addressing Satan, then we should be all the more careful when we address or discuss celestial beings—regardless of whether they represent God's angels or fallen angels. We should exhibit a certain level of respect toward them. The Bible tells us that we will judge angels (1 Corinthians 6:3); this may mean that we will judge fallen angels, or that we will exercise some authority over the angelic beings in heaven. Yet there is no place for pride on our part. Humility characterized our Lord as he lived his life on earth. It should be the same with us.

Jude concludes this point in **verse 10**: "Yet these people slander whatever they do not understand, and the very things they do understand by instinct—as irrational animals do—will destroy them." The false teachers did not have authority over these celestial beings, nor did they understand how they operate or how the spiritual battle is fought. So they slandered them and pretended to have authority over them.

Animals carry out actions not because they understand the reason for doing so but because they follow impulses and instincts. Likewise, these false teachers did not understand what they were doing. They understood by instinct that there were celestial beings, but they did not know how to properly behave toward them.

Similarly, they were led by their impulses into other immoral practices that came from their fallen and sinful instincts. **Verse 8** tells us that they "pollute their own bodies"—engaging in illicit sexual practices. They were slaves to sin with darkened minds, ignorant of the wrath of God. These false teachers were approaching the day of their judgment and final destruction like irrational animals, completely unaware of their future.

This is why Jude begins **verse 11** with the phrase, "Woe to them!" This is a pattern of speech which we find in the Old Testament (for example, in Isaiah 5:8-25). It is a curse: the opposite of a blessing. Jesus himself uses this way of speaking in Matthew 23, where he pronounces the phrase "Woe to you" seven times. Jesus is, of course, referring to false teachers. These people are cursed.

A Severe Warning

Jude now goes on to compare the false teachers with three biblical characters who serve as further examples of sin which has been judged by God (Jude **v 11**).

1. The Way of Cain

Cain famously killed his brother, Abel (Genesis 4:8). However, Jude is not implying that the false teachers were murderers. It is more likely that he is pointing out that these false teachers have rebelled against the same God that Cain rebelled against. The key moment in Cain's story was not the murder of Abel but the offering of grain he made to God (4:3-5). The Lord refused Cain's offering because his heart was not right with God (Hebrews 11:4); but instead of repenting, Cain became angry with his Creator. That is what happens to us when things do not turn out the way we expected. We become angry—and our anger is really directed toward God, who has allowed those circumstances in our lives. If someone confronts me regarding the condition of my heart and I become angry instead of repenting, I am taking "the way of Cain." I may not murder my brother, but I am still guilty.

God said to Cain, "If you do what is right, will you not be accepted?" (Genesis 4:7). But Cain did not change his ways. He continued in his rebellion, rejected God's standards, and murdered his brother. The false teachers of Jude's day rejected God in the same way. They set their own standards and did not seek to do what was right. They acted as if they were self-sufficient. That is "the way of Cain."

2. Balaam's Error

As we saw on pages 62-64, Balaam started out as one of God's prophets. He was visited by Balak, the king of the Moabites, who asked Balaam to curse the Jewish people in return for money. Balaam revealed his greed when he toyed with Balak's monetary offer. Similarly, the false teachers are motivated by "profit." Instead of putting God's word first, they are rushing to see what they can gain.

Even though money can be very beneficial, unfortunately our fallen hearts frequently succumb to its seductive power. Money tends to compete with God for first place in our lives. Money can buy security, power, pleasure, position, fame, approval, companionship—and the list goes on; and the problem is that even if God has been the provider of the riches, little by little we begin to trust the gift rather than the Giver. Balaam's error is a strong reminder to all of us not to fall into that trap.

3. Korah's Rebellion

This is a story narrated in Numbers 16, where Korah, along with 250 leaders of the people, came before Moses and Aaron and challenged their authority. He was saying that anyone could come close to God, not just the leaders whom God had appointed. In other words, Korah did not acknowledge those whom God had placed in authority over him.

Nowadays, in Christ, we all have access to God. But this story is still relevant because God has continued to establish patterns of authority: governments over citizens, husbands over wives, parents over children, and pastors and elders over believers (see Ephesians 5:21 – 6:9; 1 Peter 2:11 – 3:7). When these patterns of authority are violated, our rebellion is not ultimately aimed at the person who holds authority over us. No, God considers this to be rebellion toward himself, because he is the one who designed and delegated the authority to be carried out under his lordship. Such rebellion is nothing more than an expression of human pride and a cry by creatures for independence from their Creator. In our rebellion, we say to God that we have decided to follow a path in accordance with *our* own wisdom, and we diverge from the path that he has prepared. We think that we have a better understanding than God of the paths we should take.

God caused the earth to open and swallow up Korah and two other ringleaders, along with their entire families. Then fire came down from the heavens and consumed the 250 leaders who had risen up against Moses.

Do not speak ill of your brother or sister, who is part the people of God. Do not cause division, and do not rebel against the authorities whom God has placed over you. Otherwise, you are going the way of Korah.

Six Metaphors

Jude has finished describing the behavior of the false teachers of his time using comparisons with Old Testament figures. Now he uses six metaphors to show what they are like inside. This is a way of helping his readers understand at a deeper level how evil these people are.

1. Blemishes

Jude describes them in **verse 12** as "blemishes"—or "hidden reefs" (ESV) or "dangerous reefs" (NLT), which would be an accurate translation, since these people are capable of shipwrecking one's life. A ship could suddenly crash against unseen reefs that are beneath the water and end up shipwrecked. By allowing themselves to be led by the teachings of these false teachers, many who profess to follow Jesus have been shipwrecked. How can we avoid this? By comparing the teaching we hear with what God has revealed—as the Bereans did when they heard Paul for the first time (Acts 17:11).

> These people are capable of shipwrecking one's life.

If they did that to the apostle Paul, I would hope that we would do the same with each preacher whom we hear.

Jude says that the false teachers were "eating with [them] without the slightest qualm." These "love feasts" were the suppers the believers regularly ate together—which became, in later centuries, more formal celebrations of the **Lord's Supper**, such as we have in today's church services. When the apostle Paul wrote to the Corinthians, he reminded them of the importance of examining their consciences before partaking in the Lord's Supper (1 Corinthians 11:27-30). The Lord's Supper is an acknowledgment of what Jesus has done for us; so the Lord takes it very seriously when we partake in it while living a life of sin.

Worst of all is that these false teachers did that fearlessly—"without the slightest qualm". When we lose the fear of God, it is evidence that our conscience has become calloused and numb. The harder our conscience, the more evil we become, since we are rendered incapable of experiencing shame, guilt, or fear of sin.

2. Greedy Shepherds

Next, Jude describes the false teachers as "shepherds who feed only themselves" (**v 12**). These false teachers had probably reached positions of authority, perhaps as pastors (a word which originally meant "shepherd")—but they would use the flock for their personal benefit instead of caring for the sheep. It is possible that these false teachers made their flock participate in immoral sexual acts with them. Such acts would only worsen their coming judgment.

3. Empty Clouds

The next picture that Jude uses to describe these teachers is "clouds without rain, blown along by the wind." Palestine, where Jude probably grew up, has always been an arid place. Imagine living in that region and watching clouds come your way; yet when they arrive, they do not drop a single drop of water on the ground but continue on their way, blown by the wind. These false teachers possessed a certain similarity to those clouds. Perhaps they spoke a lot and with much fanfare, but they had nothing truthful to say because they neither knew the word of God nor his will. Their teachings and their lives were totally sinful. They had no life-bringing water to give.

4. Dead Trees

Jude keeps adding color to his description of these charlatans. Next they are "autumn trees, without fruit and uprooted—twice dead." Christ taught that "by their fruit you will recognize them" (Matthew 7:16)—and false teachers can be known by their absence of fruit. But they are even more lifeless than that; they are not only "without fruit" but also "uprooted." Uprooted trees are usually trees that have been blown down by winds; their roots have been exposed or fully torn out from the ground. This is why Jude says that such trees

are "twice dead." They are without fruit and without roots; therefore, they have no hope of flourishing. Likewise, the false teachers are without fruit and are uprooted because they are not firmly
planted in the word of God.

Something similar can happen to Christians who start to distance
themselves from God and begin to live a life of sin. Suddenly, they are
without fruit and, even worse, their lives are no longer rooted in the
word of God but instead in their sins. Jude says that when someone
reaches this point, it is as if they were dead.

5. Wild Waves

In the next metaphor, "they are wild waves of the sea, foaming up
their shame" (Jude **v 13**). Jude compares the false teachers to the
waves of a raging sea; they make a lot of noise when they crash upon
the rocks, but the noise does not produce any benefit. Similarly, false
teachers can make a lot of noise without it resulting in any benefit for
their sheep. Their shameful acts are compared to the foam that waves
leave on the rocks to be seen by everyone.

Those waves, no matter how wild they may be, end up undone as
they crash on the rocks. This is how the lives of the false teachers will
end up, too.

6. Wandering Stars

Jude's final metaphor is "wandering stars." He is talking about what
we would call shooting stars: star-like lights which we see in the
sky for a brief moment before they disappear. These are meteorites,
which are destroyed by heat upon reaching the earth's atmosphere
and quickly disappear. False teachers, too, will be quickly destroyed.
Jude concludes by stating what awaits this group of false believers
and teachers: they are those "for whom blackest darkness has been
reserved forever" (**v 13**).

Questions for reflection

1. In what ways are you tempted to follow the ways of Cain, Balaam, or Korah?

2. How do you respond to Jude's descriptions in verses 12-13?

3. Do you think that false teachers know that they are false; or do you think that they truly believe they are trying to help people? What's the biblical evidence for your view?

PART TWO

The Lord Is Coming

Jude goes on to cite an apocryphal book called Enoch. This was probably written during the time between the final book of the Old Testament and the start of the New Testament. The mention of "Enoch" (Jude **v 14**) refers to 1 Enoch; this is worth mentioning since there are other apocryphal books that bear his name: 2 Enoch and 3 Enoch. These books are neither part of the Jewish biblical canon nor part of the New Testament, but they were accepted by many Christians of the early church.

Enoch is a biblical figure; he appears in Genesis 5, where we see a series of Adam's descendants. After each one is mentioned, it says that he lived a certain number of years and then died. It is as if death reigned from one generation to another—until we get to the seventh generation (Genesis 5:21-24). Here, it is as if *life* reigned. We are told that Enoch became the father of Methuselah at the age of 65. After the birth of Methuselah, Enoch walked faithfully with God for 300 years. Then, suddenly, he disappeared one day because "God took him away". Enoch was one of those that Hebrews 11:38 refers to when it says, "the world was not worthy of them." It is as if to say that these individuals walked so rightly with God that the world is not worthy of having them remain on this side of eternity. Hebrews 11:5 tells us that the reason God took Enoch suddenly to heaven was that "he was commended as one who pleased God."

This was the Enoch who was believed, in Jude's time, to have written the Book of Enoch. He was thought to be a Christ-like figure: someone who prefigured the Messiah. Today, all scholars agree that the Book of Enoch is not inspired Scripture. However, Jude does want us to listen to its words—at least the ones he quotes here.

The use of apocryphal information in Jude has caused much debate over the years. One reason for the controversy regarding the canon of Scripture is the fact that we do not have within the body of biblical literature a list of all the books which were inspired by God. Ultimately, the canon was determined by a process carried out first by Jewish rabbis and then by the leaders of the early church. About 250 years before Christ, there was already an almost universal consensus regarding which books should be included in the Old Testament. With the New Testament, there was a much longer and more heated discussion regarding which books should be considered as inspired. At last, in AD 397, the Council of Carthage recognized as canonical all 27 books of our current version of the New Testament.

We should not consider the practice of quoting from apocryphal literature as an anomaly:

"There is nothing unusual in biblical writers referring to or quoting books that are not in our Bibles. In the Old Testament we find references to 'the Book of the Wars of the Lord', the records of Nathan the prophet and of Gad the seer, the annals of the kings of Israel and the annals of the kings of Judah."

(R.C. Lucas and Christopher Green, *The Message of 2 Peter and Jude,* Kindle loc. 3189 of 5326)

Similarly, in the New Testament, Paul quotes one of the Cretan prophets (Titus 1:12) and in Acts 17: 27-28, Paul quotes from two pagan poets and philosophers when he addresses an audience in Athens.

This should help us understand why Jude felt free to use apocryphal literature that apparently had a wide acceptance among the community of faith—Jews and Christians alike. The *Assumption of Moses* (which Jude refers to in **verse 9**), 1 Enoch, and other similar books were apparently well known by the Jewish community and by the Christian church. God inspired Jude somehow to know that this information quoted by him was reliable and important to communicate to the rest of the church—even though these books as a whole were not part of Scripture.

Jude tells us that Enoch prophesied about "ungodly sinners" such as these false teachers:

"See, the Lord is coming with thousands upon thousands of his holy ones to judge everyone, and to convict all of them of all the ungodly acts they have committed in their ungodliness, and of all the defiant words ungodly sinners have spoken against him."

(Jude **v 14-15**)

This is consistent with what is revealed to us in Revelation 19:14, where we are told that when the Lord comes to judge the world, he will come accompanied by "the armies of heaven." Daniel 7:10 speaks about the Lord on the throne of judgment, where he is accompanied by "thousands upon thousands." Zechariah 14:5 speaks of something similar. Likewise, Matthew presents a similar account in 16:27, 24:30-31, and 25:31.

This day of judgment has been planned since the beginning of time. As Jude himself said in verse 4, the false teachers' "condemnation was written about long ago." God's plan is to reveal all the evil deeds which have been done throughout history, and bring justice to everyone.

A Weighty Condemnation

Jude now goes on to conclude his description of the false teachers. **Verse 16** is weighty, as it reveals their immorality in four different ways:

1. *They Are "Grumblers and Faultfinders."* We can see how God evaluates the spirit of grumbling in Numbers 14. The Israelites are in the desert, and they grumble against Moses and Aaron, saying, "If only we had died in Egypt! Or in this wilderness!" (v 2). Note that from an earthly perspective, the protest was against Moses and Aaron. But from above the sun, God sees grumbling differently. In verse 27 he asks, "How long will this wicked community grumble against *me*?" (emphasis added). He took the complaint against Moses and Aaron as a complaint against himself. Listen to his answer: "As surely as I live, declares the LORD, I will do to you the very thing I heard you say: In this wilderness your bodies will fall— every one of you twenty years old or more who was counted in the census and who has grumbled against me" (v 28-29).

Like the Israelites in the desert, the false teachers are "grumblers and faultfinders." It is really no different with many of God's children today. Complaining is synonymous with ingratitude; we grumble in spite of everything that God has done in and for us. Brothers and sisters, when we complain, our grumbling is not really against people but against God. He has placed those people in our paths to work in our lives.

2. *"They Follow Their Own Evil Desires."* This implies that these people satisfy their lusts.

3. They *"Boast About Themselves."* False teachers boast about their power, their authority, their knowledge, and their position—all in order to impress others and intimidate the sheep. This is a far cry from the gentle and humble character of our Lord Jesus Christ.

4. They *"Flatter Others for Their Own Advantage."* The purpose of flattery is to please others in order to obtain benefits for themselves. The NLT says, "They flatter others to get what they want." These people are **narcissistic**, self-centered, and concerned only about their own interests and gains.

Sadly, these characteristics describe many people throughout the centuries and particularly in our own generation, which has been described as the generation of entitlement in the midst of a narcissism epidemic (Jean Twenge and W. Keith Campbell, *The Narcissism Epidemic*).

Time to Remember

Jude again reminds us of the need to remember the things that we have learned: "Remember what the apostles of our Lord Jesus Christ foretold" (**v 17**). By writing this way, Jude is excluding himself from the group of the apostles. He acknowledges that he was not one of them. But he does remind us that apostles like Peter, John, Paul, and others had written or taught about the same thing as him: the existence of certain individuals who do not fear God but who speak in his name while all the time trying to lead believers away from the truth.

What is the reason for calling us to remember? As time goes by, what we learned at the beginning of our walk seems to grow old and to lose relevance in our lives. Forgetting God's commandments is a common human experience. Nevertheless, it is inexcusable.

If we forget the truth of God that we learned in the past, we will drift away from God's path, slowly but surely. Almost all turning away from the faith takes place one degree at a time. It frequently begins with a doubt, then a subtle change in belief, followed by an attitude change, and finally by a new lifestyle far different from the way we once lived.

Paul Tripp provides an excellent illustration of this in his book *Lead* (pages 102-103). Imagine a person who gains half a pound in weight per month. The difference would not be noticeable at the end of the first month or even by the end of the first six months— just three pounds more—but by the end of the year, the person will have gained about six extra pounds. Perhaps the added weight would begin to show by then. If this pattern of weight gain continued for ten years, the person would look unrecognizable! This is a great illustration of how we drift in our faith and in the way we live. From barely noticeable beginnings, we end up living in ways that make us unrecognizable. People will barely believe that we are the same person they knew before.

> From barely noticeable beginnings, we can end up unrecognizable.

For this reason, Jude calls us to remember what the apostles taught.

Pause for a moment and think: what commandment or teaching have you forgotten lately? What consequences has this brought upon you? What was it that pulled you away from the truth? There are many things that can play the role of "false teacher" in our lives, leading us into deceptions:

1. *The Pattern of This World:* The apostle Paul speaks to us about not conforming to the pattern of this world and calls us to resist doing so by the renewal of our minds (Romans 12:2).

2. *Deceiving Spirits:* The same Paul warned his younger disciple, Timothy, to be on the alert and avoid being swept away by deceiving spirits (1 Timothy 4:1-16). How these spiritual beings operate is not something we can discern very well, but we are warned in Ephesians 6:12 by a veteran theologian who wrote, "For our struggle is not against flesh and blood, but against the rulers, against the authorities, against the powers of this dark world and against the spiritual forces of evil in the heavenly realms."

3. *Our Own Hearts:* The prophet Jeremiah teaches us to be careful about our own sinfulness lest we be deceived: "The heart is deceitful above all things and beyond cure. Who can understand it?" (Jeremiah 17:9). We tend to believe our hearts because they represent who we are. Our hearts feel, and this leads us to believe that our feelings define reality. But the truth is that reality is life as God sees it and not as we feel it. Feelings are real, of course, but they do not define reality for us.

   Have you been led astray by any of these things? Today is a good day to remember the truth and return to the throne of grace "so that we may receive mercy and find grace to help us in our time of need" (Hebrews 4:16).

Final Descriptions

In **verse 19**, Jude teaches us yet another consequence of having these false teachers around: they "divide you."

How do they cause division? They teach doctrines with distorted interpretations in a man-centered way to ears itching to hear them. This leads to disagreement between true believers. In our day, some people have embraced a wrong understanding about doctrine, believing that it causes division and that it is better not to teach it in case people disagree. In reality, doctrine does not divide; false teachings do. Sound doctrine should be what brings the Lord's flock together.

Jude characterizes these individuals as people "who follow mere natural instincts and do not have the Spirit" (**v 19**). These people were mocking the faith, the return of Christ, and his lordship, all the while speaking in God's name—so it was obvious that they lacked the Spirit. They did not belong to the family of God. 1 Corinthians 12:3 is helpful here: "Therefore I want you to know that no one who is speaking by the Spirit of God says, 'Jesus be cursed,' and no one can say, 'Jesus is Lord,' except by the Holy Spirit."

These false teachers demonstrated that they did not have the Spirit of God in several ways:

- By their false teachings.

- By their immoral lifestyles, which led the sheep to practice immorality.

- By their lack of self-control.

- By rejecting Christ's lordship.

They ignored what the Lord taught his disciples in Matthew 18:6-7: "If anyone causes one of these little ones—those who believe in me—to stumble, it would be better for them to have a large millstone hung around their neck and to be drowned in the depths of the sea. Woe to the world because of the things that cause people to stumble! Such things must come, but woe to the person through whom they come!"

Questions for reflection

1. We rarely talk about a man or a woman who "walks with God" rather than "believing in God." What does the word "walk" add?

2. How can you tell who is likely to lead you astray, according to verses 16-19?

3. How important to you is being doctrinally grounded? What reputation does the word "doctrine" have in your church?

9. THE ONE WHO KEEPS US FROM STUMBLING

As we saw in chapter 7, Jude's reason for writing his letter is found in verse 3: "Dear friends, although I was very eager to write to you about the salvation we share, I felt compelled to write and urge you to contend for the faith that was once for all entrusted to God's holy people." Everything written from this point on is linked to our need to contend for the faith given to all the saints once and for all.

Jude's words in verses 5-19 are shocking. Comparing false teachers with irrational animals and calling them ignorant unbelievers was as offensive then as it is now. The Old Testament prophets did it no differently; the prophet Amos, for example, called the powerful women of his time "cows of Bashan" (Amos 4:1). Those sent by God were always highly sensitive toward sin. They were always willing to expose people's failures and to call them to a higher standard of living—as Jude does. But this is motivated by love. Although Jude is very severe against the false teachers, he is at the same time sensitive and tender toward the believers.

In **verse 20**, Jude calls his readers "dear friends." Words like these have already been used several times in this epistle:

- In verse 1, Jude refers to his readers as "loved in God."

- In verse 3, Jude again calls them "dear" when he challenges them to contend for the faith.

■ In verse 17 he uses the term "dear friends" again when he calls them to remember the apostles' teaching.

This tenderness is very different from the way he describes the false teachers! The contrast is especially clear in **verses 17-19**, where Jude calls the false teachers followers of "mere natural instincts," having just addressed his readers as "dear friends."

The apostle Paul wrote to the Corinthians, "Who is weak, and I do not feel weak? Who is led into sin, and I do not inwardly burn?" (2 Corinthians 11:29). Jude, too, burns for our Lord's truth and against false teachers, feeling weighed down by the situation he is confronting. He is constantly concerned for the path Christ's sheep will take and is desperate to help them to contend for the faith without falling. This is what we see in his final verses.

How to Contend for the Faith

Before Jude finishes his letter, he seeks to leave a word of instruction to his readers regarding how to contend for the faith. His first recommendation is that they should be "building [themselves] up in [their] most holy faith" (**v 20**). This is a call to grow in our faith both as individuals and within the Christian community—which is why the NLT translates this verse by telling us to "build each other up."

One of the most important ways in which we can be built up in faith is by listening to the word. According to Ephesians 4:11-13, Christ gave his church "pastors and teachers, to equip his people for works of service, so that the body of Christ may be built up ... attaining to the whole measure of the fullness of Christ." We can neither mature nor be formed in the image of God, if we disregard God's provision of gifted teachers to instruct his people. The lack of spiritual maturity in many of God's children is nothing more than a lack of knowledge of his word and how to apply it. Although knowledge is not enough on its own to make us grow, we cannot grow without it. We also need to be filled by the Spirit so that we may put into practice what we learn.

The second recommendation that Jude makes is "praying in the Holy Spirit." Although the Bible does not give us clear instruction on how to pray in the Spirit, it should be clear to us that we should pray in accordance with the word of God and in such a way that our petitions and hopes align with God's revealed will. When we pray, we are not praying for our will to be done in heaven; that is not what our Lord Jesus Christ taught us. Instead we pray that the will of heaven may be done on earth. Through prayer in the Spirit, the Spirit of God "works in you to will and to act" (Philippians 2:13). When we pray, God places in us the desire to do the things to which he is calling us—and then gives us the ability to carry them out.

We are also told that "the Spirit himself intercedes for us through wordless groans" (Romans 8:26). As someone said on one occasion, "When God does not answer our prayers, he answers the prayer that we should have made."

The third recommendation Jude makes is to "keep yourselves in God's love." This is the only verb in the imperative—the only one that is a direct command. Jude is telling us that keeping ourselves in God's love is not an option.

This is something we ourselves need to take responsibility for. God loved us from before the foundation of the world, and we are able to love him because he loved us first. However, our Lord Jesus Christ taught us clearly in John 15:10 that "if you keep my commands, you will remain in my love, just as I have kept my Father's commands and remain in his love." John himself tells us in 1 John 3:24 that "the one who keeps God's commands lives in him, and he in them." Clearly, the way we remain in God's love is by obeying his commandments. D.A. Carson puts it the following way:

> "God remains among us and in his people by renewing them with his life, with His Spirit, and making his presence known in them and among them (John 14:16, 23); they remain in him by obeying his commandments."

(The Gospel According to John, p 516-7)

The fourth recommendation Jude makes is as follows: "Wait for the mercy of our Lord Jesus Christ to bring you to eternal life." Jude calls us to persevere as we wait for the second coming of our Lord Jesus Christ—when we will encounter his mercy. At that time, God will reward every one of us.

How to Deal with Sinners

On the other hand, while contending for the faith, we will encounter those who do not have the same degree of faithfulness towards the Lord. Jude instructs us what to do with misbehaving sheep. Once more, he creates a triplet (**v 22-23**).

1. Those Who Are Weak

Jude first calls us to have mercy on those who doubt. I recently had the opportunity to speak to a group of high-school students. At the end of my message, two different students came up to me to ask, "How do I know if I am saved?" These are those on whom Jude calls us to have mercy. It is also very possible that Jude is also thinking of those who were doubting due to the false teachings of these immoral unbelievers. Jude calls us to have patience with and mercy on such doubters.

2. Those at High Risk of Falling Away

Verse 23 names a second group of sheep: those who must be saved "by snatching them from the fire." The people in this group have apparently fallen prey to the false teachers and are about to become apostate. They have perhaps started to show signs of distancing themselves from the Christian community. Jude's recommendation is for the church to be willing to snatch them "from the fire." We are to go out looking for them and do everything within our power to try to get them to return. We will spare no effort or words in trying to call them back to the path.

This too is a call to have mercy—but more active effort is required. We are to go out looking for them wholeheartedly. Paul did this when he shepherded the church at Ephesus, and he later told the elders of that church to do the same: "So be on your guard! Remember that for three years I never stopped warning each of you night and day with tears" (Acts 20:31). Paul's words demonstrate his deep concern for Christ's sheep, but also show us that his tears did not prevent him from correcting their sinful patterns of behavior. Paul understood that warning and disciplining believers (in an open and accountable way) is vital to maintaining the church's holiness and the spiritual health of the sheep. It may be painful both to give and to hear such serious warnings, but it is the way to avoid even greater consequences.

But Paul gave his warnings with tears in his eyes. We are not told why Paul cried while he warned, but I can imagine that it pained him that saved people were not working out their salvation with "fear and trembling" (Philippians 2:12). He cried when he saw unbelievers being indifferent to the truth of the gospel and God's love in Jesus Christ. He cried after seeing people hear the gospel and understand the truth, and yet become apostate and end up in hell.

> Paul gave warnings – but with tears in his eyes.

It is extremely painful when someone who has served with you or has worshiped with you no longer wants to hear anything about the gospel. I have lived through that experience more than once, and I cannot get used to it. It rightly weighs us down when this happens.

The Puritan George Swinnock said, "If I am afraid to tell people about their sins, I murder their souls" (cited in J. Stephen Yuille, *A Labor of Love*, p 27). Paul was a pastor with a very thick skin and a very big heart. Even though he had thick skin, he very often shed many tears due to the spiritual condition of the sheep. I think he was simply following Jesus' example. Mark 6:34 highlights how Jesus felt about the people he ministered to: "When Jesus landed and saw a large crowd, he had compassion on them, because they were like sheep without a shepherd." Jesus also wept on at least one occasion as he considered the spiritual state of Jerusalem (Luke 19:41). The pastor who has never cried for his sheep needs to ask God to make his heart grow to the stature of Christ's heart.

It is an enormous responsibility to take care of the flock. This is why Jude says we need to have mercy on those sheep who doubt and are about to leave the flock. This is why he tells us that we must run after those who are about to get burned and that we need to snatch them from the fire. Scholars agree that this refers to fire from hell.

3. Those Who Are Living in Sin

Jude considers a third group of sheep in **verse 23**. He tells us, "To others show mercy, mixed with fear—hating even the clothing stained by corrupted flesh." There are believers who are living in sin, likely induced by those same leaders whom Jude calls false teachers. Jude is warning us that when we go out to their rescue, we need to be careful so that we ourselves do not fall into the sin in which they are involved.

This is why Paul tells the elders of the church at Ephesus, "Keep watch *over yourselves* and all the flock of which the Holy Spirit has made you overseers. Be shepherds of the church of God, which he bought with his own blood" (Acts 20:28; emphasis added). Paul's first call in this verse is for pastors to be careful with themselves—which is another way of saying that we need to protect our lives as we seek to cultivate holiness. The first reason we should do this is because we are not immune to any of the sheep's sins, and we are at risk of falling into immorality, as has happened so many times. The second reason is that pastors have been made overseers by the Holy Spirit. God himself called us to care for his flock. The third reason is that we are caring for sheep purchased by the blood of Christ, which is not a small responsibility.

Consequently, Jude exhorts us to be careful when we go out to rescue sheep who are already living in sin. The NLT says it this way:

"Show mercy to still others, but do so with great caution, hating the sins that contaminate their lives."

Jude has told us that we need to...

■ build ourselves up in our holy faith (**v 20**).

■ pray in the Spirit (**v 20**).

■ keep ourselves in God's love (**v 21**).

■ await our Lord Jesus Christ's mercy (**v 21**).

■ have mercy on those who doubt (**v 22**).

■ save others by snatching them from the fire (**v 23**).

■ be merciful even with those that are in sin, being careful and seeking to help them with reverent fear (**v 23**).

Finally, having instructed us in so many different ways, Jude seeks to place the emphasis where it should be, which is on "the pioneer and perfecter of faith" (Hebrews 12:2): Jesus Christ. This is where we turn in the final verses.

Questions for reflection

1. What steps can you take to build up yourself and others in faith? How can you seek to make prayer a more fundamental part of your life?

2. Do you see yourself as a sheep strong in the faith or as one who may belong to one of the three groups mentioned on pages 135-138? What help do you need?

3. How does looking forward to the mercy of Christ help you in your day-to-day life?

PART TWO

Jude ends his letter with one of the greatest doxologies in the entire Bible and even in church history. According to the *Holman Illustrated Bible Dictionary*, a doxology is "a brief formula for expressing praise or glory to God. Doxologies generally contain two elements, an ascription of praise to God … and an expression of His infinite nature." Doxologies usually appear at the end of a New Testament letter or at the end of a major section within a letter—like the one which closes Romans 11.

Jude has used 21 verses to denounce false teachers, their heretical teaching, and their damaging influence. But he now turns his masterful use of vocabulary away from man's sinfulness and toward the glory of the Creator God. There are two main themes. The first is what God is capable of doing for us, as described in Jude **v 24**. The second is related to the honor that we owe to that great God, in **verse 25**.

Powerful to Keep Us

Verse 24 says that God "is able to keep you from stumbling and to present you before his glorious presence without fault and with great joy." Our God is powerful in guaranteeing our salvation.

Hebrews 1:3 tells us that the entire *universe* is sustained "by his powerful word." But as he does this, he never tires—as he declares in Isaiah 40:28: "The LORD is the everlasting God, the Creator of the ends of the earth. He will not grow tired or weary." When God works, it does not cost him any effort. He speaks, and things take place. All of the physical forces of the universe depend on God's power in order to continue in operation.

Every second our sun converts about 700 million tons of hydrogen into approximately 695 million tons of helium, as well as 5 million tons of energy. That is about 386 billion billion megawatts per second. One second of sun energy could supply the United States with enough energy to last nine million years. This is the energy or power of just one single star—and there are 20 billion trillion stars in the universe, according to scientists! All of that energy depends on the power of our God. He sustains this universe by the power of his word, day by day, minute by minute, second by second, all without growing tired. His power is inexhaustible.

That is the God who sustains and keeps you and me from stumbling.

But what does the phrase "keep you from stumbling" mean, exactly? Of course, a Christian is capable of falling into sin and suffering great consequences. We know this because we have the example of King David in the Old Testament and the example of the apostle Peter in the New Testament—just to mention two of many in the biblical record, without counting church history. Then there is the teaching of the book of Hebrews, which tells us how God, in his goodness, disciplines his children when we disobey (Hebrews 12:4-11). So when Jude says that God has the power to keep us from stumbling, he is not saying that Christians will not fall into sin at all. He is referring to the fact that God keeps us from losing our salvation.

If someone is genuinely born again, Christ himself has guaranteed that person's salvation. Jesus said that no one could snatch the sheep out of his Father's hand (John 10:29). Therefore, "neither death nor life, neither angels nor demons, neither the present nor the future, nor any powers, neither height nor depth, nor anything else in all creation, will be able to separate us from the love of God that is in Christ Jesus our Lord" (Romans 8:38-39). It is in this sense that God keeps us from falling.

But that is not to say that his power does not work to help us stay away from sin. The Holy Spirit dwells inside believers in order to keep us. Here are some of the ways in which he does so:

- He illuminates our understanding so that we may understand Scripture and avoid veering off from the truth when false teachers or our own hearts try to deceive us.

- He works in us "to will and to act in order to fulfill his good purpose" (Philippians 2:13). Without the work of the Spirit, we would be lost because we would not be able to act righteously on a consistent basis. When we resist the Spirit, we are unable to carry out his will.

■ He produces the fruit of the Spirit in us. One of those is self-control (Galatians 5:22-23), which allows us to resist temptation. God does not allow any temptation to come our way which we would not be able to resist (1 Corinthians 10:13). But we still need his help. If I am not walking in the Spirit and I am not walking in the truth, I will not be able to count on the filling of the Spirit. Without that, we lack self-discipline, and without self-discipline we stumble and fall.

■ He produces the conviction of sin in us (John 16:8).

Finally, if we decide to continue sinning despite the conviction that the Spirit has produced, the Lord figures out a way to bring a measure of discipline into our lives, in order to open our eyes. This was the case in David's life when the prophet Nathan confronted him with his sin. Needing to be confronted in this way does not mean that you are not saved. It is your repentance at that point that speaks to the fact that you are a true believer.

The Lord disciplined the believers of the church at Corinth when some of them partook in the Lord's Supper in an unworthy manner. As a consequence, God allowed some of them to become sick or weak; in the case of others, he even took their lives (1 Corinthians 11:29-30). When the Lord takes severe action regarding one of his children in order to bring him or her to the path of righteousness (because they have not responded to his mercy), even that severe treatment is part of his grace. He is seeking to avoid bigger consequences for us. God's warnings range from a little whisper to a thunderous shout, to use the language of C.S. Lewis:

> God's warnings range from a whisper to a thunderous shout.

"God whispers to us in our pleasures, speaks in our conscience,
but shouts in our pains: it is His megaphone to rouse a deaf
world." (*The Problem of Pain*, Kindle loc. 58 of 106)

In the end we will be presented before God "without fault." If we are
truly born again, Christ brings us to the Father as people who have
been cleansed by his blood. We will come into the presence of his
grand glory "with great joy," rather than with trembling and fear—
because on that day, we will not be clothed in our holiness but in the
holiness of Christ. Moses was not able to see God's glory, but we will
see it in all of its splendor (2 Corinthians 3:7-18). It will be a day of
celebration in the heavens!

If this is where we are heading, we should make every effort to lead
a life worthy of this calling: a life of true godliness. This is not in order
to earn God's love or approval, but because we already have it. When
it comes to describing what it means to live a holy life, no one could
do a better job than the 19th-century bishop J.C. Ryle:

"Holiness is the habit of being of one mind with God … it is the
habit of agreeing in God's judgment, hating what he hates,
loving what he loves, and measuring everything in this world by
the standard of His word." (*Holiness*, p 57)

The Only God

Given what God has done for us, Jude ends with the following
words: "To the only God our Savior be glory, majesty, power and
authority, through Jesus Christ our Lord, before all ages, now and
forevermore! Amen."

These are words of praise for "the only God" of the entire universe. There have always been people who believe that there is more
than one god, but if that there were true, God would not be sovereign; his power and authority would be divided. Imagine a country
with more than one president. There would be chaos! In fact, no one

is equal to God, no one is above him, and no one has given him advice to make the decisions he has made.

Jude says that this one and only God is also our Savior. He has...

- taken us from darkness into his light.

- taken us from the lies we believed to the truth.

- taken us from shame to glory.

- taken us from slavery to freedom.

- transformed us from rebels into worshipers.

- transformed us from enemies to friends and even his children.

- transformed us from illegitimate offspring to his legitimate children.

This one and only God is our Savior. God intervened in history in a way that none of us would or could have done; he took his Son's life to give life to us, who were dead in sins and trespasses (Romans 3:20-26; Ephesians 2:1-5). He poured out his wrath upon his own Son to give us grace (2 Corinthians 5:21). He applied his justice to his Son in order to apply his mercy to us.

This God called us from eternity past and predestined us to be remade in accordance with the image of his Son. He justified us and will glorify us in himself. For this and much more, Jude says, "To him ... be glory"!

Glory, Majesty, Power, Authority

What exactly does Jude mean when he says, "Glory, majesty, power and authority"?

The word "glory" in Hebrew is *kabot*, which signifies:

- something weighty.

- something of great consideration.

■ something special and worthy of the most high reverence and adoration.

The universe is, simply because God is. To use a technical term, God is the *necessary being* in all of creation. He is the Creator of humanity's story. He began history and will end the story. History points to him and revolves around him. When something glorifies God, it reveals or acknowledges this. The story of redemption will glorify his name—as will the history of even the most secular nation. The redeemed will glorify his mercy, and the condemned will glorify his justice. In the end, everyone will glorify the God we worship!

God's glory is all that he is. Bruce A. Ware, a professor at Southern Baptist Theological Seminary, says, "The glory of God is everything that His being reflects from the inside out and His glory is also everything that His creation reflects back to Him. Creation is like a mirror that reflects the glory of the God that created it. When you look in a mirror, it receives your image and when your image is reflected in the mirror, the image returns to you. Likewise, God's glory is projected on the creation and the creation acts like a mirror, returning that same glory to God. Since every good thing that happens in the world is the result of God's work, which includes (especially) the goodness that results from human choice and action, it is logical that God receives all glory for the goodness that takes place" (*God's Greater Glory*, p 103).

Attributing all glory to God is recognizing that he deserves all the credit and glory, not only for the greatness of his being but also because he is the author of all that is good, marvelous, great, and extraordinary that exists in every corner of the universe.

To honor this God appropriately, it is not enough to do so with words alone. As Gene Green says in his commentary about Jude, it is possible "to recognize his 'honor' and pervert his ways" (*Jude and 2 Peter*, p 137). This may seem inconceivable, but unfortunately it is something that false teachers do all the time.

This God, who is described as "weighty," cannot be trivialized. Consequently, Jude attributes to our God "majesty, power, and authority."

- His majesty speaks of his greatness and splendor as King.

- His power speaks of his sovereignty.

- His authority speaks of the need that all creatures have to submit to our God.

In his book *The Attributes of God* (p 27), A.W. Pink describes our God as someone who is "subject to none, influenced by none, absolutely independent; God does as He pleases, only as He pleases, always as He pleases. None can thwart him, none can hinder Him ... Divine sovereignty means that God is God in fact, as well as in name, [and] that He is on the Throne of the universe, directing all things."

Jude says that our God possesses these attributes "before all ages, now and forevermore!" Jude is seeking to communicate that, as Gene Green puts it, "What God was before time, God is in time. His character will endure through eternity." He has been present and changeless from all eternity and will be present and changeless throughout future eternity.

This is the God of glory, majesty, sovereignty, and absolute authority: the God who is able to keep you from falling.

Amen!

Questions for reflection

1. How much of your life is intentionally dedicated to bringing glory to God?

2. What is the most amazing thing you can think of about God?

3. How can you seek holiness in your day-to-day life?

GLOSSARY

Abraham: the ancestor of the nation of Israel.

Ananias and Sapphira: in Acts 5:1-11, a couple who lied about their giving to the church and were struck dead by God.

Anomaly: a one-off.

Apocryphal: part of the Apocrypha, a set of Jewish or early Christian writings not thought to be inspired Scripture and therefore not included in the Bible.

Apostasy: the abandonment of religious belief.

Apostate: someone who once seemed to be a believer but later rejects Christ, turns away from sound teaching, and leaves the church.

Archangel Michael: a ruler among the angels, mentioned in Daniel 10:13, 21; 12:1; and Revelation 12:7. See discussion on page 116.

Ark: the boat which God ordered Noah to build, in order to be safe when God flooded the world (see Genesis 6:11-22).

Attribute: a key characteristic of someone or something.

Barnabas: a Christian in the early church who traveled alongside Paul on some of his missionary journeys.

Bathsheba: a woman with whom King David had sex, although she was not his wife at the time (see 2 Samuel 11); the mother of Solomon.

Beatitudes: Jesus' explanation of how to live in a way that is blessed. See Matthew 5:3-12 and Luke 6:20-23.

Belial: the devil.

Blaspheme: to disrespect or mock God.

Born again: having been given new, eternal life, after putting faith in Christ (see John 3:5-8; 1 Peter 1:3-5).

Canon: the set of texts which Christian tradition regards as authoritative and inspired by God. If a book is canonical, it is part of the Bible.

Church Father: one of a series of influential Christian thinkers who lived and wrote in the early centuries of the church.

Commentator: the author of a commentary, a book that explains parts of the Bible verse by verse.

Conviction: awareness of or certainty about something.

Culmination: climax or ending.

Daniel: a prophet who lived in Babylon in the 6th century BC and wrote the book of Daniel in the Old Testament. He was thrown into a den of lions because he refused to stop praying to God but was miraculously kept safe.

David: the second king of Israel, and the most important king in Old Testament history. He also wrote many of the psalms.

Doctrinal: to do with doctrine—the study of what is true about God or a statement about an aspect of that truth.

Election: being chosen by God to become his forgiven and beloved child.

Elijah: an Old Testament prophet who announced God's judgment on his people's idolatry.

Epistle: a letter.

Eschatology: the study of the end times, including what happens after death, the judgment, and the new creation.

Exorcist: someone who casts out demons.

Fall: the moment when Adam and Eve disobeyed God and ate from the tree of the knowledge of good and evil (see Genesis 3), and the consequences of that.

Father of lies: the devil.

Flesh: our natural desire to sin.

Fruit of the Spirit: the characteristics that the Holy Spirit grows in

Christians, including love, joy, peace, patience, kindness, goodness, faithfulness, gentleness and self-control (see Galatians 5:22-23).

Gnostics: the name for various religious groups in the first centuries after Christ. They thought that the material world was evil and denied that Jesus was really human.

Grace: undeserved favor. In the Bible, "grace" is usually used to describe how God treats his people. Because God is full of grace, he gives believers eternal life (Ephesians 2:4-8); he also gives them gifts to use to serve his people (Ephesians 4:7, 11-13).

Heretical: directly opposing the biblical gospel (i.e. the opposite of orthodox). A heretic is someone who, despite being challenged, continues to hold to heretical beliefs.

Heresy: a belief which directly opposes the biblical gospel.

Holy Ghost: an old term for the Holy Spirit.

Inspired: divine inspiration is the belief that all of the Bible was inspired by God, so that the humans writing the words wrote exactly what he intended them to (see 2 Timothy 3:15-17; 2 Peter 1:20-21).

Isaac: the son of Abraham and one of the "first fathers" of Israel, to whom God gave his promises.

Jeremiah: an Old Testament prophet who lived at the time Jerusalem fell to Babylonian invaders.

Jesus Movement: a movement originating in the US in the 1960s and 1970s which involved an emphasis on the miraculous power of the Holy Spirit and on evangelism. Many "Jesus people" adopted a communal lifestyle.

Job: a man who experienced great suffering despite having done nothing wrong. His story is told in the book of Job.

Jubilee: a year of celebration, resting, and restoration, which God told the Israelites to observe every fiftieth year.

Justify: declare to be innocent or right with God.

Legalistic: living by following rules, in the belief that keeping these requirements will earn blessing or salvation.

Lord's Supper: communion; sharing bread and wine together to remember the body and blood of Jesus.

Manna: the "bread" that God miraculously provided each morning for the Israelites to eat while they were journeying to the promised land (see Exodus 16). It looked like white flakes.

Metaphor: a word-image which is used to explain something, but is not to be taken literally. Metaphors describe one thing as being another thing (e.g. "The news was a dagger to his heart").

Ministry: the work of someone on behalf of God. It can include preaching and teaching about God and Jesus, and/or caring for spiritual, emotional, and physical needs.

Moses: the leader of God's people at the time when God brought them out of slavery in Egypt. God communicated his law (including the Ten Commandments) through Moses, and under his leadership guided the people toward the land he had promised to give them.

Narcissistic: extremely self-centered.

Nehemiah: a leader of God's people during the time when they left captivity in Babylon and were allowed to return to rebuild Jerusalem.

Noah: a righteous man whom God rescued, along with his family, when he flooded the world, by telling him to build an ark (see Genesis 6:11-22).

Occult: magical practices drawing on sinister supernatural powers.

Old covenant: the binding agreement which God made with his people in the Old Testament to set out how they were to relate to him. It was superseded by the new covenant, brought by Jesus.

Pagan: someone who doesn't know and worship the true God.

Pastoral: being concerned for others' welfare.

Piety: religious good deeds.

Pious: someone who prioritizes religion and doing good deeds.

Predestine: to choose what will happen in advance. God predestined

Christians to be saved, choosing us before the foundation of the world (Ephesians 1:4).

Profane: to violate or treat disrespectfully something that is sacred.

Prosperity gospel: the false teaching that God rewards faith with good health or greater wealth, and that Christians should expect and seek these things.

Reformer: one of the first two generations of people in the 15th and early 16th centuries who preached the gospel of justification by faith and opposed the Pope and the Roman church.

Revelation: when something (especially something about God) is revealed or made clear.

Saints: God's holy people—all who have been saved by Jesus.

Sanctification: the process of becoming more like Christ, by the work of the Holy Spirit.

Second coming: the day when Jesus returns to the earth to judge and rule.

Solomon: the king who succeeded David as ruler of God's people. He built the temple in Jerusalem and was renowned for his wisdom.

Stumbling: falling into sin.

Synagogue: a local place of worship, prayer, and teaching for Jewish people.

Theologian: someone who studies and writes about God.

Thomas: one of Jesus' twelve disciples, who doubted that Jesus was really alive after the crucifixion.

Trespass: sin.

Vindicate: prove right.

Wrath: God's settled, deserved hatred of and anger at sin.

BIBLIOGRAPHY

■ William Barclay, *The Letters to the Galatians and Ephesians* (WJK Press, 1958; this edition, 2017)

■ Herman Bavinck (edited by John Bolt and translated by John Vriend), *Reformed Dogmatics* (Baker Academic, 2004)

■ Jerry Bridges, *The Practice of Godliness* (NavPress, 2016)

■ John Calvin, *Commentaries on the Catholic Epistles* (Christian Classics Ethereal Library, https://ccel.org/ccel/calvin/calcom45/calcom45.vii.iv.iii.html)

■ D.A. Carson, *The Gospel According to John* (Eerdmans, 1991)

■ J. Daryl Charles, "1 & 2 Peter and Jude," in *The Expositor's Bible Commentary*, Vol. 13 (Zondervan, 2006)

■ Peter H. Davids, *The Letters of 2 Peter and Jude*, in The Pillar New Testament Commentary series (Eerdmans, 2006)

■ Mark Fackler, Linda K. Taylor, Dave Veerman, Bruce B. Barton, *1 & 2 Peter and Jude*, in the Life Application Bible Commentary series (Tyndale House, 1996)

■ Steve Farrar, *Finishing Strong: Going the Distance for Your Family* (Multnomah, 1995)

■ Norman L. Geisler, *A Popular Survey of the New Testament* (Baker, 2007)

■ Robert H. Gundry, *Commentary on the New Testament* (Hendrickson, 2010)

■ Gene L. Green, *Jude & 2 Peter* (Baker Academic, 2008)

■ James M. Hamilton Jr., *Revelation: The Spirit Speaks to the Churches,* in the Preaching the Word Commentary series (Crossway, 2012)

■ David Helm, *1 & 2 Peter and Jude: Sharing Christ's Sufferings,* in the Preaching the Word Commentary series (Crossway, 2008)

■ Kent Hughes, *Disciplines of a Godly Man* (Crossway, 1991)

■ William Law, *A Serious Call to a Devout and Holy Life* (Bridge-Logos, reprint edition, 2008)

■ C.S. Lewis, *The Problem of Pain* (HarperCollins, 2015; originally published 1940)

■ Dick Lucas, Christopher Green, *The Message of 2 Peter & Jude,* in The Bible Speaks Today series (InterVarsity Press, 1995)

■ Douglas J. Moo, *2 Peter, Jude,* in The NIV Application Bible Commentary series (Zondervan, 1996)

■ Iain H. Murray, *The Old Evangelicalism: Old Truths for a New Awakening* (Banner of Truth, 2005)

■ John Murray, *Principles of Conduct: Aspects of Biblical Ethics* (Eerdmans, 1957)

■ A.W. Pink, *The Attributes of God* (Reiner, 1968)

■ J.C. Ryle, *Holiness* (Waymark Books)

■ John Stott, *The Message of Galatians,* in the The Bible Speaks Today series (InterVarsity Press, 1988)

■ Elmer L. Towns and Ben Gutierrez, *The Essence of the New Testament: A Survey* (B & H Academic, 2012)

■ Paul David Tripp, *Lead: 12 Gospel Principles for Leadership in the Church* (Crossway, 2020)

■ Jean M. Twenge, W. Keith Campbell, *The Narcissism Epidemic: Living in the Age of Entitlement* (Atria, 2010)

- Bruce A. Ware, *God's Greater Glory: The Exalted God of Scripture and the Christian Faith* (Crossway, 2004)

- G.P. Waugh, "II Peter," in *What the Bible Teaches: 1 Peter, 2 Peter 1, 2 & 3 John, Jude,* in the Ritchie New Testament Commentaries series (John Ritchie, 2007)

- Warren Wiersbe, *The Bible Exposition Commentary* (Victor Books, 1989)

- J. Stephen Yuille, *A Labor of Love: Puritan Pastoral Priorities* (Reformation Heritage Books, 2013)

2 Peter & Jude for...
Bible-study Groups

Miguel Núñez's *Good Book Guide* to 2 Peter and Jude
is the companion to this resource, helping groups of
Christians to explore, discuss, and apply the messages
of this book together. Six studies, each including
investigation, application, getting personal, prayer and
explore more sections, take you through both books.
Includes a concise Leader's Guide at the back.

Daily Devotionals

Explore daily devotional helps you open up the Scriptures and will encourage and equip you in your walk with God. Available as a quarterly booklet, *Explore* is also available as an app, where you can download Miguel's notes on 2 Peter and Jude, alongside contributions from trusted Bible teachers including Tim Keller, Sam Allberry, Albert Mohler, and David Helm.

Find out more at:
www.thegoodbook.com/explore
www.thegoodbook.co.uk/explore

The Whole Series

- **Exodus For You** *Tim Chester*

- **Judges For You** *Timothy Keller*

- **Ruth For You** *Tony Merida*

- **1 Samuel For You** *Tim Chester*

- **2 Samuel For You** *Tim Chester*

- **Psalms For You** *Christopher Ash*

- **Proverbs For You** *Kathleen Nielson*

- **Isaiah For You** *Tim Chester*

- **Daniel For You** *David Helm*

- **Micah For You** *Stephen Um*

- **Luke 1-12 For You** *Mike McKinley*

- **Luke 12-24 For You** *Mike McKinley*

- **John 1-12 For You** *Josh Moody*

- **John 13-21 For You** *Josh Moody*

- **Acts 1-12 For You** *Albert Mohler*

- **Acts 13-28 For You** *Albert Mohler*